Teaching with Questions

Help your students navigate complex texts in social studies and across the curriculum! This book shows you how to use a key tool—text-based questions—to build students' literacy and critical thinking skills and meet the Common Core State Standards. You'll learn how to ask text-based questions about different types of nonfiction and visual texts, including primary and secondary sources, maps, charts, and paintings. You'll also get ideas for teaching students to examine point of view, write analytical responses, compare texts, cite textual evidence, and pose their own high-level questions. The book is filled with examples that you can use immediately or modify as needed. Each chapter ends with a reflection section to help you adapt the ideas to your own classroom.

What's inside:

- Helpful information on teaching different types of nonfiction texts, including literary nonfiction, informational texts, primary and secondary sources, and visual texts
- Ideas for locating primary sources
- Questions students should ask about every text
- Techniques for soliciting higher-order questions from students
- Ways to get students to think critically about the relationships between texts
- Strategies to help students integrate information from different types of sources
- Tips for teaching students to write good responses to text-based questions, including how to cite sources and incorporate point of view
- Ideas for using rubrics and peer grading to evaluate students' responses
- Connections to the informational reading standards of the Common Core State Standards for English Language Arts for grades 3–12 and of the Common Core State Standards for Literacy in History/Social Studies, Science, and Technical Subjects

Kevin Thomas Smith is a distinguished high school teacher in Florida and a frequent presenter on current topics in social studies education.

Other Eye On Education Books Available from Routledge
(www.routledge.com/eyeoneducation)

Rebuilding Research Writing
Strategies for Sparking Informational Inquiry
Nanci Werner-Burke, Karin Knaus, and Amy Helt DeCamp

Common Core Reading Lessons
Pairing Literary and Nonfiction Texts to Promote Deeper Understanding
Stacey O'Reilly and Angie Stooksbury

Big Skills for the Common Core
Literacy Strategies for the 6–12 Classroom
Amy Benjamin and Michael Hugelmeyer

Teaching the Common Core Speaking and Listening Standards
Strategies and Digital Tools
Kristen Swanson

The Common Core Grammar Toolkit
Using Mentor Texts to Teach the Language Standards in Grades 3–5
Sean Ruday

Authentic Learning Experiences
A Real-World Approach to Project-Based Learning
Dayna Laur

Vocabulary Strategies That Work
Do This—Not That!
Lori G. Wilfong

Common Core Literacy Lesson Plans
Ready-to-Use Resources, K–5

Common Core Literacy Lesson Plans
Ready-to-Use Resources, 6–8

Common Core Literacy Lesson Plans
Ready-to-Use Resources, 9–12
Edited by Lauren Davis

Helping English Language Learners Meet the Common Core
Assessment and Instructional Strategies, K–12
Paul Boyd-Batstone

Teaching Students to Dig Deeper
The Common Core in Action
Ben Johnson

Teaching with Text-Based Questions

Helping Students Analyze Nonfiction and Visual Texts

Kevin Thomas Smith

Taylor & Francis Group
NEW YORK AND LONDON

First published 2014
by Routledge
711 Third Avenue, New York, NY 10017

and by Routledge
2 Park Square, Milton Park, Abingdon, Oxon OX14 4RN

Routledge is an imprint of the Taylor & Francis Group, an informa business

© 2014 Taylor & Francis

The right of Kevin Thomas Smith to be identified as author of this work has been asserted by him in accordance with sections 77 and 78 of the Copyright, Designs and Patents Act 1988.

All rights reserved. No part of this book may be reprinted or reproduced or utilized in any form or by any electronic, mechanical, or other means, now known or hereafter invented, including photocopying and recording, or in any information storage or retrieval system, without permission in writing from the publishers.

Trademark notice: Product or corporate names may be trademarks or registered trademarks, and are used only for identification and explanation without intent to infringe.

Library of Congress Cataloging-in-Publication Data
Smith, Kevin Thomas.
Teaching with text-based questions : helping students analyze nonfiction and visual texts / Kevin Thomas Smith.
    pages cm
  Includes bibliographical references and index.
 1. Critical thinking—Handbooks, manuals, etc.   2. Test-taking skills—Handbooks, manuals, etc.   3. Teaching—Handbooks, manuals, etc.
4. Thought and thinking—Study and teaching.   5. Education—Standards.
6. Reading comprehension—Problems, exercises, etc.   7. Developmental reading.   I. Title.
LB1590.3.S55   2014
372.47—dc23   2013036811

ISBN: 978-0-415-74403-4 (hbk)
ISBN: 978-0-415-74404-1 (pbk)
ISBN: 978-1-315-81321-9 (ebk)

Typeset in Bembo
by Apex CoVantage, LLC

Printed and bound in the United States of America by Publishers Graphics, LLC on sustainably sourced paper.

For
my wife, Elizabeth

Contents

	Acknowledgments	*ix*
	Meet the Author	*xi*
	Introduction	*xiii*
1	**Why Text-Based Questions?**	**1**
	Summary	9
	References	11
2	**The Different Types of Nonfiction Text**	**13**
	Literary Nonfiction vs. Informational Text	16
	Primary Sources	17
	Secondary Sources	19
	Visual Texts	21
	Locating Primary Sources	22
	Summary	27
	References	29
3	**Questions Students Should Be Asking About Texts**	**31**
	Questions Students Should Ask About Every Text	31
	Soliciting High-Order Questions from Students	37
	Graphic Organizers for Practice	38
	The Questions Game	40
	The SOAPSTone Technique	41
	Summary	45
	References	46
4	**Working with Multiple Texts**	**47**
	Getting Students to Think Critically About the Relationship Between Texts	50
	Making Text-Based Questions Fun for Students	52
	Using the SOAPSTone Technique to Analyze Multiple Texts	57
	Comparing Two Texts Using the SOAPSTone Technique	65
	Have Students Create Their Own Text-Based Questions	69

	Integrating Information from Different Types of Sources	70
	Tips for Creating a Good Text-Based Question	75
	Summary	76
	References	78
5	**Writing Good Responses to Text-Based Questions**	**79**
	Multiple-Choice vs. Free-Response Questions	86
	Formulating a Thesis Statement	90
	Supporting the Thesis with Evidence	100
	Citing Sources	102
	Incorporating Point of View	103
	Writing a Conclusion	104
	Additional Tips	105
	Summary	107
	References	109
6	**Evaluating Students' Responses to Text-Based Questions**	**111**
	Using Rubrics to Evaluate Students' Responses	111
	Assigning Grades to Students' Work	115
	Peer Grading	116
	Summary	117
	Appendix: Common Core Exemplars for Informational Text	*119*

Acknowledgments

This book may have just one author, but there are a number of people whose knowledge, passion, and experience went into producing it. That being the case, I owe a big thank you to my editor at Routledge, Lauren Davis, for walking me through each step of the writing process and providing me with valuable feedback on the first drafts of the manuscript. I also want to thank Justin Jones and Kevin Lewis, my dearest friends and colleagues, for taking time out of their busy schedules to read, reflect, and critique each chapter. A special thank you goes out to Laura Johnson, my long-time mentor, for sharing so much of her time and wisdom with me over the years; my parents, Tom and Lorraine Smith, for being the best teachers I ever had; and my wife, Elizabeth, for reading the manuscript at least half the number of times I did and for making it a little bit better every time she touched it.

Last, but not least, I would like to thank my students for making my work in the classroom these past ten years so exciting, challenging, and rewarding. I sincerely hope that I have been able to make a difference in their lives. I know they have made a difference in mine.

Meet the Author

Kevin Thomas Smith earned his B.A. and M.A.E. from the University of North Florida in Jacksonville. During the past 10 years, Mr. Smith has taught a variety of AP subjects, including AP world history, AP European history, and AP U.S. government and politics. He has also taught a number of advanced and non-advanced courses in these subjects, as well as a course on Nazi Germany and the Holocaust. In both his school and his district, Mr. Smith is known for being a dynamic presenter, a committed scholar, an inspiring leader, and a phenomenal AP teacher. Most years, between 80 and 100 percent of his students pass their AP exams (and many students score a 4 or a 5). In 2003, as a first-year teacher, Mr. Smith was a Teacher of the Year Finalist, and in 2004, his achievements in the classroom were recognized by the Clay County Chamber of Commerce. In 2005 and 2006, the Clay County School Board recognized Mr. Smith as an exemplary teacher.

Mr. Smith's success has extended beyond the classroom. In addition to being an AP Reader for the College Board, Mr. Smith conducts workshops on text-based questions for elementary, middle, and high schools in his district. In 2012, he was invited to serve on a special task force on clinical education at the University of North Florida. His new venture, *Teaching With Text-Based Questions*, is helping educators across the country teach their students to read, think, and write analytically.

Introduction

A few months ago, I conducted a workshop at one of the elementary schools in my district. The principal, who had once been a supervisor of mine, wanted me to familiarize her teachers with text-based questions (TBQs) and show them how this type of question can be used to teach students to analyze, evaluate, and write about informational, literary nonfiction, and visual texts. While I have been using TBQs for the past 10 years with my own students for this very purpose, I was a little nervous about conducting a workshop of this kind for teachers at her school.

My nervousness did not stem from a fear of public speaking. I am used to getting up in front of people and delivering presentations. In fact, I rather enjoy being "on stage" and often jump at the chance to share my knowledge and experience with other professionals in my field. However, in this case, I had to combat feelings of inadequacy. I am a high school social studies teacher; the teachers to whom I was presenting teach students in grades K–6. While I was confident that they could use TBQs as I do to teach important literacy skills, I was not sure how to modify the activities I use with my own students so as to make them relevant and meaningful to elementary teachers.

Even though I spent many hours preparing for the workshop, the butterflies in my stomach had not disappeared by the time my car pulled into the parking lot on presentation day. In fact, even as I climbed out of my car and began heading toward the front door of the school, my palms were sweating. I could not escape the feeling that these teachers would perceive me as a less-than-credible presenter because of my high school background or feel my activities were not relevant or meaningful to them.

When I shared these concerns with the principal, she laughed and told me not to worry. She said her teachers would understand that my examples had been created solely for illustrative purposes and they would be able to modify my examples to use with their own students. She had been trying to get them to use TBQs as a method for teaching informational texts and visuals for some time, but with little success. Therefore, my greatest challenge would be to convince them that TBQs are a powerful tool for helping students meet the nonfiction requirements of Common Core.

In order to do this, however, I needed to find out what the teachers knew and thought about TBQs. I decided to kick-off the training with this very question, and their answers did not surprise me. All of them said they had heard of TBQs but admitted to knowing little about them. Most were under the impression that TBQs were only for students in high school or those taking Advanced Placement (AP) courses. That being the case, many thought TBQs were too difficult for students in "regular" classes or classes taught by elementary and middle school teachers. A few thought TBQs were too time consuming to be practical, and at least two of them believed they were already using some form of TBQs in their classrooms.

Unfortunately, these misperceptions are very common. Most of the teachers I have talked to either have not heard of TBQs or have heard of them only in connection with some AP classes. For this reason, they assume TBQs are either out of reach for their own students or are not applicable to the particular subject(s) they teach.

Fortunately, the new Common Core State Standards promise to change this. These standards, which have been formally adopted by 45 states, the District of Columbia, and four US territories so far, lay out a vision of what it means to be truly literate in the 21st century. The realization of this vision requires that students develop the skills necessary for evaluating complex texts across a range of types and disciplines and crafting sophisticated arguments supported by textual evidence (CCSSI, 2010). TBQs are a powerful, cutting-edge tool for helping students in all grades and content areas develop these skills. However, teachers currently have access to few, if any, resources that will show them how to effectively use TBQs for this purpose.

That being the case, a book of this kind is sorely needed. Its purpose is to familiarize teachers with TBQs and show them how TBQs can be used to teach important literacy skills. It includes a number of strategies for helping students learn how to navigate different types of text, work with multiple sources, analyze point of view, write analytical responses, and cite textual evidence. While each of these strategies can be used in any classroom, each of the examples I have included was created with a specific grade or subject in mind and is meant to be modified. Therefore, the examples are just a springboard from which teachers can develop and implement their own ideas for using TBQs in their classrooms.

What's Inside This Book

When I sat down at the beginning of the writing process to create an outline for this book, it made sense to me to split the book into six chapters. The first chapter focuses on defining text-based questions and convincing teachers that they are a powerful, cutting-edge tool for teaching content as well as analytical reading, thinking, and writing. In Chapter 1, I explain how TBQs are aligned with the overall mission of the Common Core State Standards and recount a part of my own journey and success with TBQs as a classroom teacher. At the end of the chapter, I include testimonials from former students who recognize the benefit of TBQs to themselves as well as testimonials from other teachers and administrators who have experienced great success with TBQs at their schools.

In Chapter 2, I focus on familiarizing teachers with the nonfiction requirements of the Common Core State Standards and explaining the difference between several broad types of nonfiction text: literary nonfiction and informational texts, visual and nonvisual texts, and primary and secondary sources. This chapter includes a section for teachers on how to locate primary sources online as well as a list of websites, organized alphabetically, that teachers can go to in order to get access to free primary sources.

In the first half of Chapter 3, I highlight specific strategies teachers can use to get students asking their own good text-based questions. The second half of the chapter focuses on helping students to organize their questions in a way that will allow them to extrapolate meaning from individual texts. In Chapter 4, I show teachers how to use TBQs to teach students to integrate and evaluate information from multiple texts. This chapter includes specific strategies for teaching students how to understand the relationship between texts (and how texts can work together to answer a question or solve a problem); compare texts; understand how one text fills in gaps left by another text; know how to integrate background knowledge with knowledge gleaned from a text; evaluate authors' differing points of view; and recognize what additional perspective(s) or types of text would be useful for exploring a topic or solving a problem.

Chapter 5 focuses on teaching students how to respond to text-based questions. In this chapter, I include specific suggestions for teaching students how to craft sophisticated arguments, formulate a thesis statement, and cite textual evidence. In Chapter 6, I talk about evaluating students' responses to TBQs and provide teachers with some generic rubrics they can use to help them with their scoring.

Finally, I have included a complete list of Common Core exemplar texts for students in grades K–12 in the appendix. These resources will undoubtedly be useful to teachers as they implement the Common Core State Standards and incorporate TBQs into their regular classroom instruction.

Reference

Common Core State Standards Initiative (CCSSI). (2010, June). *Common Core State Standards for English Language Arts & Literacy in the History/Social Studies, Science, and Technical Subjects.* Retrieved from *www.corestandards.org/ELA-Literacy*

CHAPTER 1

Why Text-Based Questions?

Even though I made "As" most of the way through grade school, I do not believe I was adequately prepared for the rigors of higher education. While I thoroughly enjoyed my K–12 experience and believe I learned a lot, much of the work I did, even in my advanced classes, was not particularly challenging. Rather than teach me to think analytically, it simply required me to regurgitate facts—facts I had acquired from reading my textbook or actively listening to my teachers' presentations. For this reason, I graduated high school with a false sense of confidence that I was ready for the challenge of a university education.

Reality hit home, however, by the end of my first day of college. In fact, I called my parents after classes to tell them that I was considering dropping out of school. The workload, I said, was too intense, and the reading was too complex. I had more reading to do in one night than I had ever done in a week during high school. Furthermore, I had a three-to-five-page paper to write by the end of the weekend (longer than any essay I had to write in high school), and a test to start studying for that would constitute 25 percent of my entire semester grade. Fortunately, my parents managed to calm me down and convince me to stay in school; after a few months of very hard work, I began to feel more confident about my ability to do well. Still, I believe there was too great a gap between the expectations of my high school teachers and the demands placed on me by my university professors.

Perhaps if I had taken more AP classes in high school, I would not feel this way. My AP English class, which I took as a junior, was the one most closely aligned with college-level expectations. Our reading assignments were diverse, and our essay prompts required at least a shred of analytical thinking. Books we read included *The Scarlet Letter* (Hawthorne, 1850), *A Separate Peace* (Knowles, 1959), *As I Lay Dying* (Faulkner, 1930), and *The Great Gatsby* (Fitzgerald, 1925). While we read other classic works of literature in my other English classes, such as *Silas Marner* (Eliot, 1861), *The Canterbury Tales* (Chaucer, 1400), and *Romeo and Juliet* (Shakespeare, 1597), I do not remember reading anything but the textbook in any of my other subjects.

Looking back, I should have taken more AP classes when I was in high school. Even though some of the courses offered now, such as AP human geography and AP world history, did not exist then, there were plenty of other AP classes for me to choose from. However, at that time, I naturally assumed that a high school education consisting mostly of honors classes would mirror the expectations of university professors and more than adequately prepare me for college.

I suspect a lot of students today assume this as well. I know my own students, including students in my non-advanced courses, talk about college as if it will simply be an extension of their high school education. They talk about going to the University of Florida and other universities in our state as if their academic experiences at these schools will closely resemble their high school experiences. In fact, students sometimes complain about the work they are expected to do in my classes, asking if they will ever have to do this much (and this kind of) intellectual work in college.

I cannot help but chuckle, at least on the inside, whenever my students ask me this question, especially when they insinuate that kids these days are being made to work so much harder and "be so much smarter" than students were when I went to high school almost 15 years ago. Because I do not want to make them feel bad, I do not tell them that there is a lot of evidence to suggest that students today are not working harder, and are not any smarter, than they were 15 or 30 years ago. If anything, they are falling behind their peers in other parts of the world. For example, the United States currently ranks 25th in math and 21st in science among 30 developed countries. When the comparison is restricted to the top 5 percent of students, the United States ranks last. In 1970, the United States produced 30 percent of the world's college graduates. Today, however, it produces only 15 percent. Since 1971, education spending in the United States has more than doubled from $4,300 per student to more than $9,000 per student. Yet reading and math scores have remained flat in the United States, even as they have risen in virtually every other developed country (Weber, 2010).

There are several reasons for this disparity in student achievement. First, students do not possess the skills they need to compete globally in the 21st century. In his book *The Global Achievement Gap* (2008), Tony Wagner identified seven important skills our schools are not currently teaching. These skills, which include critical thinking and problem solving, effective oral and written communication skills, and accessing and analyzing information, are a must-have for the future. Yet, sadly, only 1 in 20 classes in our nation's best schools are teaching them. Second, schools are narrowing their curriculum in order to show progress on state tests that emphasize math and reading. Instructional resources are being diverted toward these subjects and away from subjects such as art, music, foreign language, and social studies (Farkas Duffet Research Group, 2012). Third, students are becoming increasingly lazy. According to Thomas Friedman (2005), American students do not work as hard as students in other countries. This is especially true when American students are compared to students in countries like Finland, Singapore, Korea, and China (Darling-Hammond, 2010).

Additionally, each state in our country has developed its own standards for measuring student achievement. What a student is expected to know in Idaho, for example, is not necessarily what a student is expected to know in Florida. Furthermore, the standards developed by individual states during the past two decades are primarily content driven and are generally not as rigorous as standards in other developed countries. On the other hand, the Common Core State Standards are internationally benchmarked to ensure that students are college- and career-ready and can compete with their peers around the globe. Instead of being content driven, the Standards emphasize the development of *skills* students need to be truly literate in the 21st century—the same skills Wagner said our schools *should* be teaching. While content will always be important, we, as teachers, must stop making content coverage our primary focus and focus instead on teaching these skills.

In the past, the responsibility for teaching literacy skills fell almost exclusively on English teachers. Today, the expanding concept of literacy requires that teachers in all grades and content areas share this responsibility. Teaching these skills will certainly be a challenge, considering many K–12 students have been raised on a system that has not emphasized critical thinking. Therefore, if we expect all students to master the Common Core grade level and anchor standards before graduation (see Figure 1.1), we must develop and use effective tools for teaching content as well as analytical thinking and writing.

Text-based questions are such a tool. Broadly defined, TBQs are questions that can only be answered by referring back to the text. While not all TBQs require high-order thinking, good TBQs require students to analyze and evaluate what they are reading and support their responses with strong textual evidence. Unlike questions that require students to recall factual information, good TBQs integrate skills with content and facilitate a deeper reading of texts. More complex TBQs require students to work with multiple sources written from different points of view and understand how those sources work together to answer a question. While background knowledge may be useful to

Common Core Anchor Standards for Reading

Key Ideas and Details

S1: Read closely to determine what the text says explicitly and to make logical inferences from it; cite specific textual evidence when writing or speaking to support conclusions drawn from the text.
S2: Determine central ideas or themes of a text and analyze their development; summarize the key supporting details and ideas.
S3: Analyze how and why individuals, events, and ideas develop and interact over the course of a text.

Craft and Structure

S4: Interpret words and phrases as they are used in a text, including determining technical, connotative, and figurative meanings, and analyze how specific word choices shape meaning or tone.
S5: Analyze the structure of texts, including how specific sentences, paragraphs, and larger portions of the text (e.g., a section, chapter, scene, or stanza) relate to each other and the whole.
S6: Assess how point of view or purpose shapes the content and style of a text.

Integration of Knowledge and Ideas

S7: Integrate and evaluate content presented in diverse formats and media, including visually and quantitatively, as well as in words.
S8: Delineate and evaluate the argument and specific claims in a text, including the validity of the reasoning as well as the relevance and sufficiency of the evidence.
S9: Analyze how two or more texts address similar themes or topics in order to build knowledge or to compare the approaches the authors take.

Range of Reading and Level of Text Complexity

S10: Read and comprehend complex literary and informational texts independently and proficiently.

Common Core Anchor Standards for Writing

Text Types and Purposes

S1: Write arguments to support claims in an analysis of substantive topics or texts using valid reasoning and relevant and sufficient evidence.
S2: Write informative/explanatory texts to examine and convey complex ideas and information clearly and accurately through the effective selection, organization, and analysis of content.
S3: Write narratives to develop real or imagined experiences or events using effective technique, well-chosen details and well-structured event sequences.

Production and Distribution of Writing

S4: Produce clear and coherent writing in which the development, organization, and style are appropriate to task, purpose, and audience.
S5: Develop and strengthen writing as needed by planning, revising, editing, rewriting, or trying a new approach.
S6: Use technology, including the Internet, to produce and publish writing and to interact and collaborate with others.

Figure 1.1 Common Core Anchor Standards for Reading and Writing
Source: CCSSI, 2010

Research to Build and Present Knowledge

S7: Conduct short as well as more sustained research projects based on focused questions, demonstrating an understanding of the subject under investigation.
S8: Gather relevant information from multiple print and digital sources, assess the credibility and accuracy of each source, and integrate the information while avoiding plagiarism.
S9: Draw evidence from literary or informational texts to support analysis, reflection, and research.

Range of Writing

S10: Write routinely over extended time frames (time for research, reflection, and revision) and shorter time frames (a single sitting or a day or two) for a range of tasks, purposes, and audiences.

Figure 1.1 (*Continued*)

students for answering the question, their answers must always be supported with evidence from the text.

Even though school districts around the country are just now beginning to encourage the use of TBQs in all K–12 classes to teach analytical thinking and writing skills and meet the nonfiction requirements of Common Core, TBQs have been around for quite some time. Since 1973, the College Board has been using a form of TBQs, called document-based questions (DBQs), on its AP history examinations to assess students' ability to work with historical documents (including primary sources). The creators of the DBQ, Giles Hayes and Stephen Kline, were unhappy with students' answers to free-response questions. Like the thematic essays typically assigned to high school students in non-AP courses, these questions allowed students to parrot back information with little historical analysis or argument. The purpose of creating the DBQ was to make students less concerned with factual recall and more concerned with getting students to think and write like historians (Henry, n.d.).

Today, TBQs make up part of the AP U.S. history, AP world history, AP European history, and AP English language and composition exams as well as the history exams given by the International Baccalaureate (IB) and Advanced International Certification of Education (AICE) programs. They are also a part of the New York Regents Examinations in U.S. history and government and global history. However, TBQs are not just for high school students, students in advanced classes, or those taking history courses. They are useful to students in all grades and subjects. In fact, what makes TBQs such an effective and versatile tool is their ability to be used by teachers in all grades and content areas to teach students how to analyze, evaluate, and write about informational, literary nonfiction, and visual texts. They can be written for any subject, be about any topic, and incorporate as many different types of sources (written from as many different points of view) as teachers choose. They can be easily incorporated into regular classroom instruction and can be completed individually, in small groups, or as a class.

My own journey with TBQs began during my first year of teaching. After completing my internship and graduating from college in the spring of 2003, I was hired to teach AP world history and world history honors at a brand new high school in northeast Florida. Because my experience teaching AP courses was obviously very limited (I taught AP human geography during internship but under the supervision of a directing teacher), my principal sent me to a week-long training that summer in Atlanta, Georgia.

Despite having read the 100-page course description for AP world history before leaving for Atlanta, I arrived at the training with very little knowledge about TBQs. Fortunately, most of the other teachers at the training knew little about TBQs as well, so our instructor spent a lot of time on them. A few hours each day were spent looking at TBQs, discussing them as a group, and grading sample student responses. By the time the training was over, I felt I had a better understanding of what I was supposed to cover in the course as well as how TBQs were supposed to be read and scored.

What I did not have, however, were resources I could use for teaching TBQs. While I obviously had copies of the TBQs we used during the training, these were not enough. In order for my students to get sufficient practice working with TBQs, I was going to need at least a dozen more. Furthermore, I was going to need something easier than any of the TBQs we were given at the training. These TBQs were truly AP caliber—that is, they were as challenging as the TBQs students would see on the AP exam in May. Given that this was August, I was going to need something simple to start with. Over time, of course, the TBQs could become increasingly challenging.

I looked online for what I needed; but, unfortunately, there was nothing—nothing, at least, that I could use at the end of August as opposed to May. That being the case, I set to work creating my own TBQs. Starting with the Neolithic Revolution and ending with the collapse of the Soviet Union, I created more than 20 TBQs for use in AP world history—TBQs that got progressively more challenging as the year went on.

At the same time, I began developing effective strategies for teaching my students the skills they needed to complete TBQs successfully. For example, I developed specific techniques for getting my students to ask questions of their reading (the first step toward analysis) and for distinguishing one type of text from another. I developed strategies for teaching point of view and understanding the relationship between sources. I taught them to formulate a thesis statement, write analytical essays, and cite textual evidence. I got them thinking about what points of view were missing from the texts and to suggest additional texts they thought would be helpful. While these strategies were—and still are—a work in progress, they served their purpose. By the end of the year, my students' skill set had improved dramatically. Not only could they navigate different types of text and write analytical essays, their vocabularies, I noticed, had significantly improved, and they made fewer spelling and grammatical errors.

When my students' AP scores came back in July, the results supported the growth I had witnessed during the year. Eighty-three percent of my students passed the exam with a 3, 4, or 5—the highest percentage in the entire school. The next year, the results were even better: 92 percent of students passed the exam. In 2005, I took on an AP European history class in addition to AP world history and had 100 percent of my students pass that exam.

Obviously, I was very proud of my students' success. However, I was beginning to wonder if I should use TBQs in my honors classes as well. Just because I had used TBQs in my AP classes first did not mean they were off-limits to students in my non-AP courses. Therefore, I began incorporating TBQs into my honors classes the following year—and, when I changed schools in 2008, into my non-advanced courses as well. Like many of the students in my AP classes, my non-AP students required significant scaffolding at first. Over time, however, they began to think and write much like the students in my AP courses.

While I was obviously aware of the progress my students were making, my students were well aware of their progress as well. In addition to AP scores, which validated the efforts of my AP students, students in all my classes said that TBQs made them better readers, writers, and thinkers. They said TBQs helped them to write better essays for FCAT Writes, our state's writing assessment, as well as for the SAT, ACT, and college placement exams. Ultimately, they felt that TBQs made them better students, increased their confidence, and prepared them for college.

Over the years, many of my students have come back to thank me for the work they did with TBQs. My desk drawer at home is filled with cards and letters I have received from grateful students. I have also received letters from teachers and administrators about the positive impact TBQs are having at their school. Here are just a few of the positive comments:

> *TBQs have helped me improve my writing skills. In the beginning, they threw me out of my comfort zone. As time went on, however, I learned how to manage my time, know precisely what the prompt was asking, and get into an analytical mindset. I learned how to write a solid thesis statement and group texts properly.*

Not only did these skills help me in my AP World History class, they have come in handy as I take on more rigorous courses that require the same level of writing excellence.

—Leah Ayres
Former High School Student

By using TBQs, the teachers at my school have been able to inspire their students to grapple with and construct meaning from highly complex text. Students are taught, through the use of TBQs, to think critically in order to analyze details from multiple sources and can support their final conclusions by specific evidence from these readings. TBQs provide a sturdy underpinning for and an effective instrument to assist in the achievement of the Common Core State Standards. I have every confidence that the use of TBQs will raise student achievement on high stakes tests.

—Laura Johnson
Elementary School Principal

TBQs were to my learning experience as shredded cheese is to a bowl of chili: absolutely necessary. When asked to analyze a document, I'm being asked to think about information and not to just regurgitate facts. Throughout my further education in history, my ability to analyze various documents has contributed to a deeper, more personal understanding of the subject. Prior to my awareness of TBQs, I assumed that history was a sea of knowledge miles wide and an inch deep. With the tools to analyze documents, I feel that I am more able to understand and remember information.

—Jane Stanley
Former High School Student

My class is comprised of students with Specific Learning Disabilities, a student with Asperger Syndrome, and two with cochlear implants and significant language delays. These students struggled with higher-order thinking as evidenced by their extreme difficulty in interpreting inferential style questions. They had difficulty explaining how they arrived at the answers to which they correctly responded and had more difficulty defending their answers in writing. Even though I make it daily practice to have the students identify the specific text within passages to support their answers, they had never used text to defend their own unique perspective and develop their argument by citing the text. With the implementation of TBQs with my students, I found that they were more engaged in the text because they knew they had to answer questions critically and find specific information to be able to support their arguments. They have made great gains in identifying crucial from non-crucial details that are relevant to their answers. I believe they are beginning to understand the subtleties in texts as they search for deeper meaning. It is only a beginning, and we have much work to do, but the progress is promising.

—Carrie Dean
Third Grade Inclusion Teacher

These comments remind us that TBQs are for teaching skills as well as content and are not just for regular ed students. They are for all students, including students with special needs and those learning to speak English as a second language. They also remind us that teaching skills is a process—not something we do overnight. TBQs are a powerfully effective tool for improving literacy, but they are not a magic bullet. Like any other tool, they must be used deliberately and expertly, and in conjunction with other strategies, if we want to maximize their effectiveness. They must be incorporated into classroom instruction on a regular basis throughout the school year. That being the case, the time to start is now. The work will be long and challenging, but the results will be worth the effort.

Summary

Today's students do not possess the skills they need to compete globally in the 21st century. In addition to not working as hard as students in many other countries, students in the United States are not performing as well on standardized assessments. For example, the United States currently ranks 25th in math and 21st in science among 30 developed countries. When the comparison is restricted to the top 5 percent of students, the United States ranks last. During the last 30 years, reading and math scores have remained flat in the United States, but they have risen in virtually every other developed country (Weber, 2010).

In his book *The Global Achievement Gap* (2008), Tony Wagner identified seven important skills our schools are not currently teaching. These skills, which include critical thinking and problem solving, effective oral and written communication skills, and accessing and analyzing information, are a must-have for the future. Yet, sadly, only 1 in 20 classes in our nation's best schools are teaching them. Also, schools are narrowing their curriculum in order to show progress on state tests that emphasize math and reading. Instructional resources are being diverted toward these subjects and away from subjects such as art, music, foreign language, and social studies (Farkas Duffet Research Group, 2012).

Each state in our country has developed its own standards for measuring student achievement. What a student is expected to know in Idaho, for example, is not necessarily what a student is expected to know in Florida. Furthermore, the standards developed by individual states during the past two decades are primarily content driven and are generally not as rigorous as standards in other developed countries. On the other hand, the Common Core State Standards are internationally benchmarked to ensure that students are college- and career-ready and can compete with their peers around the globe. Instead of being content driven, the Standards emphasize the development of *skills* students need to be truly literate in the 21st century—the same skills Wagner said our schools *should* be teaching. While content will always be important, we, as teachers, must stop making content coverage our primary focus and focus instead on teaching these skills.

In the past, the responsibility for teaching literacy skills fell almost exclusively on English teachers. Today, the expanding concept of literacy requires that teachers in all grades and content areas share this responsibility. Teaching these skills will certainly be a challenge, considering many K–12 students have been raised on a system that has not emphasized critical thinking. Therefore, if we expect all students to master the Common Core grade level and anchor standards before graduation, we must develop and use effective tools for teaching content as well as analytical thinking and writing.

Text-based questions are such a tool. Broadly defined, TBQs are questions that can only be answered by referring back to the text. While not all TBQs require high-order thinking, good TBQs require students to analyze and evaluate what they are reading and support their responses with strong textual evidence. Unlike questions that require students to recall factual information, good TBQs integrate skills with content and facilitate a deeper reading of texts. More complex TBQs require students to work with multiple sources written from different points of view and understand how those sources work together to answer a question. While background knowledge may be useful to students for answering the question, their answers must always be supported with evidence from the text.

TBQs are a powerful, cutting-edge tool for teaching skills as well as content and are not just for regular ed students. They are for all students, including students with special needs and those learning to speak English as a second language. However, while TBQs are a powerfully effective tool for improving literacy, they are not a magic bullet. Like any other tool, they must be used deliberately and expertly, and in conjunction with other strategies, if we want to maximize their effectiveness. They must be incorporated into classroom instruction on a regular basis throughout the year.

How are you currently asking students to respond to a text? How might your students benefit from text-based questions? Feel free to jot down some of your thoughts and ideas here:

_____
_____
_____

References

Common Core State Standards Initiative (CCSSI). (2010, June). *Common Core State Standards for English Language Arts & Literacy in the History/Social Studies, Science, and Technical Subjects.* Retrieved from www.corestandards.org/ELA-Literacy

Chaucer, G. (1400 [1951]). *The Canterbury Tales* (trans. N. Coghill). London: Penguin Books.

Darling-Hammond, L. (2010). *The Flat World and Education: How America's Commitment to Equity Will Determine Our Future.* New York: Teachers College Press.

Eliot, G. (1861). *Silas Marner.* Edinburgh: William Blackwood and Sons.

Farkas Duffet Research Group (2012). *Learning Less: Public School Teachers Describe A Narrowing Curriculum.* Retrieved from http://commoncore.org/reports

Faulkner, W. (1930). *As I Lay Dying* (1st Vintage international ed.). New York: Vintage Books.

Fitzgerald, F.S. (1925). *The Great Gatsby.* Scribner.

Friedman, T.L. (2005). *The World Is Flat.* New York: Farrar, Straus, and Giroux.

Hawthorne, N. (1850). *The Scarlet Letter.* Boston: Ticknor, Reed, and Fields.

Henry, M. (n.d.). *The DBQ Change: Returning to the Original Intent.* Princeton: The College Board. Retrieved from http://apcentral.collegeboard.com/apc/members/homepage/10467.html

Knowles, J. (1959). *A Separate Peace.* New York: Scribner.

Shakespeare, W. (1597 [2004]). *Romeo and Juliet.* New York: Simon and Schuster.

Wagner, T. (2008). *The Global Achievement Gap.* New York: Basic Books.

Weber, K. (Ed.) (2010). *Waiting for Superman: How We Can Save America's Failing Schools.* New York: Perseus Book Group.

CHAPTER 2

The Different Types of Nonfiction Text

Even though I did a lot of reading when I was growing up, especially at home and in my English/language arts classes, most of what I read consisted of literary fiction. Even in my AP English class, which best prepared me for college, I read only works of fiction. In my other subjects, I rarely read anything, mainly because I was able to make "As" in school without doing the required reading. (This was not so much due to my brilliance as a student as to the general lack of rigor in my K–12 education.) However, even when I did have to read, at home or in class, the only nonfiction I can ever remember reading were my textbooks.

Yet, as an adult, most of what I have been required to read, both in college and on the job, has been nonfiction, including informational texts. Since I have always enjoyed reading fiction (and believe there is a lot of recreational and intellectual value in doing so), I manage to sneak some fiction onto my reading list each year—usually during the summer when I am not busy teaching. For the most part, however, I read books like this one—books that are meant to convey information rather than tell a story.

Today's high-skill jobs require employees to work with increasing amounts of nonfiction, especially informational text. Since the importance of images and visual media are changing the way we define literacy, the word *text* now encompasses a wide variety of print and electronic media. In the future, employees will need to integrate and evaluate media presented in diverse formats, including visually and qualitatively, in order to compete globally. For this reason, the Common Core State Standards place greater emphasis on nonfiction, including informational and visual texts, than individual states have in the past. While English/language arts classes will still get a healthy dose of fiction, the Standards say that the amount of fiction students read should decrease as they get older. For example, in grade 4, students should be reading about the same amount of fiction as nonfiction. By grade 12, however, approximately 70 percent of the curriculum should consist of nonfiction titles. This means that the vast majority of what students read in their social studies, science, mathematics, and technical subjects (art, music, and other electives) should be nonfiction. In their English classes, students should be doing a fair bit of nonfiction reading as well (CCSSI, 2010).

Common Core Connection

ELA Literacy Standards for Informational Text

Grade 3
RI.3.7: Use information gained from illustrations (e.g., maps, photographs) and the words in a text to demonstrate understanding of the text (e.g., where, when, why, and how key events occur).
RI.3.10: By the end of the year, read and comprehend informational texts, including history/social studies, science, and technical texts, at the high end of the grades 2–3 text complexity band independently and proficiently.

Grade 4
RI.4.6: Compare and contrast a first-hand and second-hand account of the same event or topic; describe the differences in focus and the information provided.
RI.4.7: Interpret information presented visually, orally, or quantitatively (e.g., in charts, graphs, diagrams, time lines, animations, or interactive elements on Web pages) and explain how the information contributes to an understanding of the text in which it appears.
RI.4.10: By the end of the year, read and comprehend informational texts, including history/social studies, science, and technical texts, in the grades 4–5 text complexity band proficiently, with scaffolding as needed at the high end of the range.

Grade 5
RI.5.7: Draw on information from multiple print or digital sources, demonstrating the ability to locate an answer to a question quickly or to solve a problem efficiently.
RI.5.10: By the end of the year, read and comprehend informational texts, including history/social studies, science, and technical texts, at the high end of the grades 4–5 text complexity band independently and proficiently.

Grade 6
RI.6.7: Integrate information presented in different media or formats (e.g., visually, quantitatively) as well as in words to develop a coherent understanding of a topic or issue.
RI.6.9: Compare and contrast one author's presentation of events with that of another (e.g., a memoir written by and a biography on the same person).
RI.6.10: By the end of the year, read and comprehend literary nonfiction in the grades 6–8 complexity band proficiently, with scaffolding as needed at the high end of the range.

Grade 7
RI.7.7: Compare and contrast a text to an audio, video, or multimedia version of the text, analyzing each medium's portrayal of the subject (e.g., how the delivery of a speech affects the impact of the words).
RI.7.10: By the end of the year, read and comprehend literary nonfiction in the grades 6–8 text complexity band proficiently, with scaffolding as needed at the high end of the range.

Grade 8
RI.8.7: Evaluate the advantages and disadvantages of using different mediums (e.g., print or digital text, video, multimedia) to present a particular topic or idea.

Figure 2.1 Common Core Literacy Standards for Informational Text
Source: CCSSI, 2010

RI.8.10: By the end of the year, read and comprehend literary nonfiction at the high end of the grades 6–8 complexity band independently and proficiently.

Grades 9–10
RI.9–10.7: Analyze various accounts of a subject told in different mediums (e.g., a person's life story in both print and multimedia), determining which details are emphasized in each account.
RI.9–10.10: By the end of the year, read and comprehend literary nonfiction in the grades 9–10 text complexity band proficiently.

Grades 11–12
RI.11–12.7: Integrate and evaluate multiple sources of information presented in different media or formats (e.g., visually, quantitatively) as well as in words in order to address a question or solve a problem.
RI.11–12.10: By the end of the year, read and comprehend literary nonfiction in the grades 11–CCR text complexity band proficiently.

History/Social Studies Literacy Standards for Informational Text

Grades 6–8
RH.6–8.1: Cite textual evidence to support analysis of primary and secondary sources.
RH.6–8.2: Determine the central ideas or information of a primary or secondary source; provide an accurate summary of the source distinct from prior knowledge or opinions.
RH.6–8.7: Integrate visual information (e.g., in charts, graphs, photographs, videos, or maps) with other information in print and digital texts.
RH.6–8.9: Analyze the relationship between a primary and secondary source on the same topic.
RH.6–8.10: By the end of grade 8, read and comprehend history/social studies texts in the grades 6–8 text complexity band independently and proficiently.

Grades 9–10
RH.9–10.1: Cite specific textual evidence to support analysis of primary and secondary sources, attending to such features as the date and origin of the information.
RH.9–10.2: Determine the central ideas or information of a primary or secondary source; provide an accurate summary of how key events or ideas develop over the course of the text.
RH.9–10.7: Integrate quantitative information or technical analysis (e.g., charts, research data) with qualitative analysis in print or digital texts.
RH.9–10.9: Compare and contrast treatments of the same topic in several primary and secondary sources.
RH.9–10.10: By the end of grade 10, read and comprehend history/social studies texts in the grades 9–10 text complexity band independently and proficiently.

Grades 11–12
RH.11–12.1: Cite specific textual evidence to support analysis of primary and secondary sources, connecting insights gained from specific details in the texts to an understanding of the text as a whole.
RH.11–12.2: Determine the central ideas or information of a primary or secondary source; provide an accurate summary that makes clear the relationship among the key details and ideas.
RH.11–12.7: Integrate and evaluate multiple sources of information presented in diverse formats and media (e.g., visually and quantitatively, as well as in words) in order to address a question or solve a problem.
RH.11–12.9: Integrate information from diverse sources, both primary and secondary, into a coherent understanding of an idea or event, noting discrepancies among sources.
RH.11–12.10: By the end of grade 12, read and comprehend history/social studies texts in the grades 11-CCR text complexity band independently and proficiently.

Figure 2.1 (*Continued*)

Science and Technical Subjects Literacy Standards for Informational Text

Grades 6–8
RST.6–8.7: Integrate quantitative or technical information expressed in words in a text with a version of that information expressed visually (e.g., in a flowchart, diagram, model, graph, or table).
RST.6–8.9: Compare and contrast the information gained from experiments, simulations, video, or multimedia sources with that gained from reading a text on the same topic.
RST.6–8.10: By the end of grade 8, read and comprehend science/technical texts in the grades 6–8 text complexity band independently and proficiently.

Grades 9–10
RST.9–10.9: Compare and contrast findings presented in a text to those from other sources (including their own experiments) noting when the findings support or contradict previous explanations or accounts.
RST.9–10.10: By the end of grade 10, read and comprehend science/technical texts in the grades 9–10 complexity band independently and proficiently.

Grades 11–12
RST.11–12.7: Integrate and evaluate multiple sources of information presented in diverse formats and media (e.g., quantitative data, video, multimedia) in order to address a question or solve a problem.
RST.11–12.8: Evaluate the hypotheses, data, analysis, and conclusions in a science or technical text, verifying the data when possible and corroborating and challenging conclusions with other sources of information.
RST.11–12.9: Synthesize information from a range of sources (e.g., texts, experiments, simulations) into a coherent understanding of a process, phenomenon, or concept, resolving conflicting information when possible.
RST.11–12.10: By the end of grade 12, read and comprehend science/technical texts in the grades 11–CCR text complexity band independently and proficiently.

Figure 2.1 (*Continued*)

Literary Nonfiction vs. Informational Text

Of course, like the word *fiction*, which refers to a wide variety of literature (short stories, poetry, historical fiction, fables, folk tales, myths, legends, and drama), *nonfiction* encompasses a wide variety of factual (or, at least, assumed to be factual) texts. While the words *nonfiction* and *informational* are often used interchangeably, they are not the same. Informational text is a type of nonfiction. Its purpose is to convey information about the natural or social world to the reader. On the other hand, *literary nonfiction* is a genre of writing that uses literary styles and techniques to create factually accurate narratives. Unlike informational texts, which include expository and functional texts, literary nonfiction tells a story (albeit a factual one). Examples of informational texts include newspaper and research articles, encyclopedia entries, textbooks, diagrams, maps, charts, graphs, political cartoons, photographs, and directions; examples of literary nonfiction include biographies, autobiographies, and personal memoirs.

Primary Sources

Literary nonfiction and informational texts are both comprised of two broad types of sources: primary and secondary. Primary sources are created by people who have first-hand knowledge of a topic or event. Primary sources can include a wide variety of nonfiction texts (including visual texts) such as diaries, letters, emails, research articles, case studies, autobiographies, personal memoirs, government documents, maps, charts, graphs, newspapers, drawings, photographs, paintings, sculptures, videos, political cartoons, manuscripts, speeches, pamphlets, oral histories, sheet music, and original audio recordings.

For instance, a newspaper article about the bombing of Pearl Harbor or the collapse of the Soviet Union is a primary source, provided it was written at the time those events occurred. Similarly, articles about childhood obesity or breast cancer research are primary sources as long as they were written by the person (or people) who conducted the research. On the other hand, autobiographies and personal memoirs are *always* primary sources, even if they are recalling events that took place many years before. The same is true of diaries, letters, and emails.

Take, for example, Christopher Columbus' description of the indigenous people he encountered when he landed on the island of Hispaniola in 1492:

> It appeared to me to be a race of people very poor in everything. They go as naked as their mothers bore them, and so do the women, although I did not see more than one young girl. All I saw were youths, none more than thirty years of age. They are very well made, with handsome bodies, and very good countenances. Their hair is short and coarse, almost like the hair of a horse's tail. They wear the hairs brought down to the eyebrows, except a few locks behind, which they wear long and never cut. They paint themselves black, and they are the color of Canarians, neither black nor white. Some paint themselves white, others red, and others of what color they find. Some paint their faces, others the whole body, some only around the eyes, others only on the nose. They neither carry nor know anything of arms, for I showed them swords, and they took them by the blade and cut themselves through ignorance. They have no iron, their darts being wands without iron, some of them having a fish's tooth at the end, and others being pointed in various ways. They are all of fair stature and size, with good faces, and well made.
>
> *Source:* Markham, C.R. (Ed.) (1893). *The Journal of Christopher Columbus (During His First Voyage, 1492–1493).* London: The Hakluyt Society.

Obviously, Columbus had first-hand knowledge of what these native people were like. He personally sailed west from Europe across the Atlantic Ocean, claimed the island of Hispaniola for Spain, and had contact with its inhabitants. This does not mean that his account does justice to the natives' true appearance or that the judgments he makes about them are not premature. Still, this diary entry constitutes a primary source because Columbus was an active participant in the events he described.

Even had Columbus written this description many years after his voyage, it would still constitute a primary source. In 1845, Frederick Douglass, a former slave, wrote his first autobiography, *Narrative of the Life of Frederick Douglass*. In this book, he recalled his life in bondage:

> I have had two masters. My first master's name was Anthony. I do not remember his first name . . . He owned two or three farms, and about thirty slaves. His farms and slaves were under the care of an overseer. The overseer's name was Plummer. Mr. Plummer was a miserable drunkard, a profane swearer, and a savage monster. He always went armed with a cowskin and a heavy cudgel. I have known him to cut and slash the women's heads so horribly, that even master would be enraged at his cruelty, and threaten to whip him if he did not mind himself. Master, however, was not a humane slaveholder. It required extraordinary barbarity on the part of an overseer to affect him. He was a cruel man, hardened by a long life of slaveholding. He would at times seem to take great pleasure in whipping a slave. I have often been awakened at the dawn of day by the most heart-rending shrieks of an own aunt of mine, whom he used to tie up to a joist, and whip upon her naked back until she was literally covered in blood. No words, no tears, no prayers from his gory victim, seemed to move his iron heart from its bloody purpose. The louder she screamed, the harder he whipped; and where the blood ran fastest, there he whipped the longest. He would whip her to make her scream, and whip her to make her hush; and not until over-come by fatigue would he cease to swing the blood-clotted cowskin.
>
> *Source:* Douglass, F. (1845). *Narrative of the Life of Frederick Douglass, An American Slave.* Boston: Anti-Slavery Office.

Like Columbus' description of the natives on the island of Hispaniola, Douglass' narrative gives a first-hand account of his life as a slave. Even though he wrote it many years after witnessing his aunt's brutal whipping, it describes an event that touched him personally.

Other examples of primary sources include the following Common Core text exemplars for history/social studies, mathematics, science, and technical subjects: *The Elements* (Euclid, 300 BCE), the *US Constitution* (United States, 1787), and *Executive Order 13423: Strengthening Federal Environmental, Energy, and Transportation Management* (United States General Services Administration, 2007). Primary sources for English/language arts include *Common Sense* (Paine, 1776), "The Gettysburg Address" (Lincoln, 1863), and "Letter on Thomas Jefferson" (Adams, 1776).

Unfortunately, all of these texts are exemplars for students in grades 6–12. While students in grades K–5 would also benefit from working with primary sources, most primary sources are not written for a young audience. However, teachers can expose young students to primary sources by using texts that have been edited so as to make them developmentally appropriate for their grade level. Take, for example, Nelson Mandela's autobiography, *Long Walk to Freedom* (1994), which was abridged by Chris Van Wyck in 2009:

> My name is Nelson Mandela. I live in South Africa, a beautiful country on the tip of Africa. Today South Africa is a democracy. That means all adults vote to choose who they want to run the country. But it was not always like this. When I was born, South Africa was ruled by white people only. As I grew older, I began to see that this was not fair. I wanted to change this way of government so everyone had a say. My friends and I called this the struggle for freedom. The struggle lasted many years, and I was one of the fighters. This is my story.
>
> *Source:* Wyck, C. (Ed.). (2009). *Nelson Mandela: Long Walk to Freedom.* New York: Flash Point Press.

While Wyck shortened Mandela's text and simplified the language, he did not change its content. Since edited texts are probably the only primary sources accessible to younger readers, this abridged autobiography can be treated as a primary source.

Secondary Sources

Secondary sources are written by people who have either studied the primary sources themselves or have read the works of others whose interpretations are based on primary research. Like primary sources, secondary sources can include a wide variety of nonfiction texts (including visual texts) such as scholarly books, review articles, textbooks, encyclopedias, magazines, biographies, charts, graphs, paintings, and pamphlets.

For instance, articles about childhood obesity or breast cancer research are secondary sources if they were written by someone other than the person (or people) who conducted the research. Similarly, books about the causes of World War I or the impact of the Civil War on the economy of the South are secondary sources because their authors rely on primary sources (and sometimes other secondary sources) for their information. Reference books, such as textbooks and encyclopedias, are secondary sources as well.

Take, for example, James C. Davis' description of Columbus' first encounter with the indigenous people of Hispaniola:

> As the ships approached the land, the sailors saw a sparkling shoreline, lofty trees and nearly naked people. The islanders feared the monsters nearing shore, and they vanished into the forest. Columbus and his men went ashore, and there they kneeled and thanked God for their safe arrival, and Columbus formally named the isle San Salvador (Holy Savior).
>
> The islanders returned, and timidly they offered gifts. Columbus, thinking he was in the "Indies", called them Indians, and he wrote that they were "poor in everything." However, some were wearing little gold pendants hanging from their noses. The Spaniards focused keenly on these pendants, and were sorry to learn that the gold had come from some other island.
>
> *Source:* Davis, J.C. (2004). *The Human Story: Our History from the Stone Age to Today.* New York: HarperCollins.

Although similar to Columbus' own description, Davis' account was not based on any first-hand knowledge of the encounter. Writing in 2004, Davis was not alive when Columbus discovered the New World. Therefore, he could not have been a member of Columbus' crew or have otherwise witnessed Columbus' first encounter with the "Indians." Davis' account was based on the writings of Columbus himself—specifically, his diary entry for October 12, 1492.

Other examples of secondary sources include the following Common Core text exemplars for history/social studies, mathematics, science, and technical subjects: *Untangling the Roots of Cancer* (Gibbs, 2008), *Math Trek: Adventures in the Math Zone* (Peterson & Henderson, 2000), and *Discovering Mars: The Amazing Story of the Red Planet* (Berger, 1992). Secondary sources for English/language arts include *Harriet Tubman: Conductor on the Underground Railroad* (Petry, 1955), *My Librarian Is A Camel: How Books Are Brought to Children Around the World* (Ruurs, 2005), and *A Weed Is A Flower: The Life of George Washington Carver* (Aliki, 1965).

Visual Texts

Like word-based texts, visual texts can be either primary or secondary sources. Visual texts include a wide variety of print and electronic media such as drawings, paintings, photographs, maps, charts, graphs, political cartoons, diagrams, and videos.

For instance, a painting of a battle scene is a primary source, provided the artist saw the battle with his own eyes. However, if the artist's rendition of the battle is based on someone else's description, then it is a secondary source. Similarly, videos made by the Allies when they liberated Nazi concentration camps at the end of World War II are primary sources; video documentaries made by others about the liberation of the camps are secondary sources (even though they may include some primary-source material). A graph showing the increasing prevalence of childhood obesity in the United States is a primary source if it was made by the person (or people) who conducted the research. However, if that same graph was created by someone else, such as a journalist compiling data from several studies, then it is a secondary source.

Take, for example, Jean-Léon Gérôme's 1842 painting *Pollice Verso* (see Figure 2.2). This painting is a secondary source because it is based on the

Figure 2.2 *Pollice Verso* by Jean-Léon Gérôme
Source: Wikipedia

artist's researched conception of gladiatorial combat. Obviously, Gérôme did not live in ancient Rome and could not have witnessed this brutal scene himself. His painting is an interpretation of historical events based on the analysis of primary-source material. On the other hand, Vincent van Gogh's 1889 masterpiece *Starry Night* (see Figure 2.3) is a primary source, because it is based on van Gogh's own impression of the view outside his bedroom window.

Locating Primary Sources

In the past, the standards adopted by individual states emphasized literary fiction over nonfiction, secondary sources over primary sources, and word-based texts over visuals. Today, the Common Core State Standards require students to become proficient at working with a wide variety of print and electronic media (including visual texts) in order to be college- and career-ready in the 21st century. This means that we, as teachers, must stop treating our textbooks as a primary source and incorporate other nonfiction texts, including *real* primary sources, into our classroom instruction. In addition to providing students with direct access to the raw materials of the subjects we teach, primary sources facilitate a deeper reading of texts than secondary sources. Primary sources develop students' critical thinking skills by requiring them to

Figure 2.3 *Starry Night* by Vincent van Gogh

Source: Wikipedia

ask questions about their reading, make inferences, and analyze point of view. Because each source represents only one person's thoughts and interpretations, students must work with multiple sources from different points of view in order to gain a more complete understanding of the topics they study.

Fortunately, there are lots of primary sources online, and many of them are free for teachers to download, copy, and use. (Generally, the fair use doctrine, which was incorporated into U.S. copyright law in 1976, allows teachers to reproduce and use copyrighted material for teaching purposes. This includes making multiple copies for classroom use.) The websites for the Library of Congress, National Archives, Smithsonian Center for Education and Museum Studies, and Federal Resources for Educational Excellence are great places for all teachers to start, but they are only a few of the many websites that offer up dozens—if not hundreds—of free primary sources. Below is a list of websites that provide free primary sources for teachers and students. While many of these websites may appear to focus solely on the study of history, it is important to remember that primary sources in math, science, and English/language arts are part of the historical record. For this reason, some history-related websites may prove very useful to elementary and secondary teachers in other content areas as well.

Ad* Access
http://library.duke.edu/digitalcollections/adaccess
Over 7,000 U.S. and Canadian advertisements covering five product categories—beauty and hygiene, radio, television, transportation, and World War II propaganda—between 1911 and 1955.

African-American Mosaic
www.loc.gov/exhibits/african/intro.html
Library of Congress website that includes primary sources related to the study of African-American history and culture.

American RadioWorks
http://americanradioworks.publicradio.org/features/prestapes/index.html
Series of audio clips recorded during phone calls in the Oval offices of John F. Kennedy, Lyndon Johnson, and Richard Nixon.

America's Story
www.americaslibrary.gov
Library of Congress website designed for younger students featuring stories of America's past.

Ancient History Sourcebook
www.fordham.edu/halsall/ancient/asbook.asp
Primary sources on the Mesopotamian, Egyptian, Greek, and Hellenistic world.

AP Central
http://apcentral.collegeboard.com/home
Website for AP teachers. Provides questions from past AP exams and other resources that include primary sources. Applicable to history, social studies, science, mathematics, English, and other subjects.

Authentic History Center
www.authentichistory.com
Primary sources from American popular culture. Over 5,000 audio, video, and text files of public speeches, sermons, legal proceedings, lectures, debates, and interviews.

Ben Franklin's Lightning Bells
http://sln.fi.edu/franklin/bells.html
Includes letters and papers written by Benjamin Franklin about his science experiments.

Census Bureau Economics Page
www.census.gov/econ/www/index.html
The U.S. Census Bureau's website includes a wide range of economic data on trade, housing, income, education, and manufacturing.

Center for Innovation and Engineering and Science Education
www.ciese.org/primarysourceproj.html
Includes primary sources for use in K–12 science education.

Chronicling America
http://chroniclingamerica.loc.gov
This website is sponsored jointly by the National Endowment for the Humanities and the Library of Congress. Includes newspaper pages published in the United States between 1690 and the present.

Common Core Text Exemplars for English/Language Arts, History/Social Studies, Science, Mathematics, and Technical Subjects *http://corestandards.org/assets/Appendix_B.pdf*

This PDF file includes Common Core exemplar texts for students in all major subjects, grades K–12. Includes some primary sources.

Digital History
www.digitalhistory.uh.edu
Primary sources about landmark events in American history.

Eyewitness to History
http://eyewitnesstohistory.com
Your ringside seat to history—from the ancient world to the present. History through the eyes of those who lived it. This website is presented by Ibis Communications, Inc., a digital publisher of education programming.

Fold3
www.fold3.com
A large collection of original U.S. military records.

FreeLunch.Com
www.economy.com/freelunch
This website provides free access to economic, industrial, financial, and demographic data.

Free Medical Journals
www.freemedicaljournals.com
Provides free access to medical journals dealing with topics related to biology, cardiology, endocrinology, infectious diseases, genetics, microbiology, neurology, oncology, physiology, and more.

Great Debates in Astronomy
http://apod.nasa.gov/diamond_jubilee/debate.html
Go to this website to view primary source documents related to major debates in the field of astronomy.

Historical Thinking Matters
http://historicalthinkingmatters.org
This website is focused on key topics in U.S. history and is designed to teach students how to critically read primary sources.

History Channel
www.history.com/speeches
Audio clips from famous speeches in American history.

Labyrinth
www.georgetown.edu/labyrinth
This website provides full-text versions of medieval documents and literature.

Last Expression: Art and Auschwitz
http://lastexpression.northwestern.edu/
Publishes and explores art made in Nazi concentration camps.

Letters of Note
www.lettersofnote.com
Collection of famous and not-so-famous letters, postcards, telegrams, faxes, and memos.

Medieval Sourcebook
http://fordham.edu/halsall/sbook.asp
Large collection of primary sources about the medieval world.

Modern History Sourcebook
www.fordham.edu/halsall/mod/modsbook.asp
Large collection of primary sources about the modern world (after 1500).

National Gallery of Art: NGA Images
http://images.nga.gov/
A repository of digital images of the collections of the National Gallery of Art. More than 25,000 images are free to download and use.

Oyez Project
www.oyez.org
Database on major constitutional cases heard by the U.S. Supreme Court, with multimedia resources including digital audio of oral arguments.

Presidential Recordings Program—Miller Center
http://millercenter.org/academic/presidentialrecordings
Five thousand hours of secret audio recordings from six American presidents: Franklin D. Roosevelt, Harry S. Truman, Dwight D. Eisenhower, John F. Kennedy, Lyndon B. Johnson, and Richard Nixon.

Primary Source Nexus
http://primarysourcenexus.org
This website integrates a variety of primary source materials from a number of different content areas, including mathematics, science, and American (including African-American and Asian-American) history.

PubMed
www.ncbi.nlm.nih.gov/pubmed
This website includes a number of full-text journal articles dealing with a wide range of health-related issues.

United States Holocaust Memorial Museum
www.ushmm.org/research/collections
Provides extensive resources, including primary sources, on the Holocaust.

Voice of the Shuttle
http://vos.ucsb.edu/browse.asp?id=2722
This website is a great place for teachers to begin their search for primary sources in any area of history.

Voices of the Holocaust
www.bl.uk/services/learning/curriculum/voices.html
British Library website that publishes audio files and transcripts of Holocaust survivor testimonies.

Summary

Today's high-skill jobs require employees to work with increasing amounts of nonfiction, especially informational text. Since the importance of images and visual media are changing the way we define literacy, the word *text* now encompasses a wide variety of print and electronic media. In the future, employees will need to integrate and evaluate media presented in diverse formats, including visually and qualitatively, in order to compete globally. For this reason, the Common Core State Standards place greater emphasis on nonfiction, including informational and visual texts, than individual states have in the past.

Like the word *fiction*, which refers to a wide variety of literature (short stories, poetry, historical fiction, fables, folk tales, myths, legends, and drama), *nonfiction* encompasses a wide variety of factual (or, at least, assumed to be factual) texts. While the words *nonfiction* and *informational* are often used interchangeably, they are not the same. Informational text is a type of nonfiction. Its purpose is to convey information about the natural or social world to the reader. On the other hand, *literary nonfiction* is a genre of writing that uses literary styles and techniques to create factually accurate narratives. Unlike informational texts, which include expository and functional texts, literary nonfiction tells a story (albeit a factual one).

Literary nonfiction and informational texts are both comprised of two broad types of sources: primary and secondary. Primary sources are created by people who have first-hand knowledge of a topic or event. Primary sources can include a wide variety of nonfiction texts (including visual texts) such as diaries, letters, emails, research articles, case studies, autobiographies, personal memoirs, government documents, maps, charts, graphs, newspapers, drawings, photographs, paintings, sculptures, videos, political cartoons, manuscripts, speeches, pamphlets, oral histories, sheet music, and original audio recordings.

Secondary sources are written by people who have either studied the primary sources themselves or have read the works of others whose interpretations are based on primary research. Like primary sources, secondary sources can include a wide variety of nonfiction texts (including visual texts) such as scholarly books, review articles, textbooks, encyclopedias, magazines, biographies, charts, graphs, paintings, and pamphlets.

In the past, the standards adopted by individual states emphasized literary fiction over nonfiction, secondary sources over primary sources, and word-based texts over visuals. Today, the Common Core State Standards require students to become proficient at working with a wide variety of print and electronic media (including visual texts) in order to be college- and career-ready in the 21st century. This means that we, as teachers, must stop treating our textbooks as a primary source and incorporate other nonfiction texts, including *real* primary sources, into our classroom instruction. In addition to providing students with direct access to the raw materials of the subjects we teach, primary sources facilitate a deeper reading of texts than secondary sources. Primary sources develop students' critical thinking skills by requiring them to ask questions about their reading, make inferences, and analyze point of view. Because each source represents only one person's thoughts and interpretations, students must work with multiple sources from different points of view in order to gain a more complete understanding of the topics they study.

Fortunately, there are lots of primary sources online, and many of them are free for teachers to download, copy, and use. The websites for the Library of Congress, National Archives, Smithsonian Center for Education and Museum

Studies, and Federal Resources for Educational Excellence are great places for teachers in all grades and content areas to start, but they are only a few of the many websites that offer up dozens—if not hundreds—of free primary sources.

How might you incorporate more primary sources into your units? Feel free to write some of your ideas here:

References

Adams, J. (1776). Letter on Thomas Jefferson. In Zall, P.M. (Ed.). (2009). *Adams on Adams*. Lexington: University of Kentucky.

Aliki. (1965). *A Weed Is A Flower: The Life of George Washington Carver*. New York: Prentice Hall.

Berger, M. (1992). *Discovering Mars: The Amazing Story of the Red Planet*. New York: Scholastic.

Common Core State Standards Initiative (CCSSI). (2010, June). *Common Core State Standards for English Language Arts & Literacy in the History/Social Studies, Science, and Technical Subjects*. Retrieved from *www.corestandards.org/ELA-Literacy*

Davis, J.C. (2004). *The Human Story: Our History from the Stone Age to Today*. New York: HarperCollins.

Douglass, F. (1845). *Narrative of the Life of Frederick Douglass, An American Slave*. Boston: Anti-Slavery Office.

Euclid. (300 BCE [2005]). *The Elements* (trans. R. Fitzpatrick). Austin: Richard Fitzpatrick.

Gibbs, W.W. (2008, June). Untangling the Roots of Cancer. *Scientific American Special Edition*.

Lincoln, A. (1863). The Gettysburg Address.

Markham, C.R. (Ed.). (1893). *The Journal of Christopher Columbus (During His First Voyage, 1492–1493)*. London: The Hakluyt Society.

Paine, T. (1776 [2005]). *Common Sense*. New York: Penguin.

Peterson, I. & Henderson, N. (2000). *Math Trek: Adventures in the Math Zone*. San Francisco: Jossey-Bass.

Petry, A. (1955 [1983]). *Harriet Tubman: Conductor on the Underground Railroad*. New York: HarperCollins.

Ruurs, M. (2005). *My Librarian Is A Camel: How Books Are Brought to Children Around the World*. Honesdale: Boyds Mills Press.

United States. (1787). *US Constitution*.

United States General Services Administration. (2007). *Executive Order 13423: Strengthening Federal Environmental, Energy, and Transportation Management*.

Wyck, C. (Ed.). (2009). *Nelson Mandela: Long Walk to Freedom*. New York: Flash Point Press.

CHAPTER 3

Questions Students Should Be Asking About Texts

Text-based questions make the different types of text (literary nonfiction and informational, primary and secondary, visual and nonvisual) accessible and relevant to students. While not all TBQs require high-order thinking, good TBQs require students to analyze and evaluate what they are reading and support their responses with evidence from the text. Unlike questions that require students to recall factual information, good TBQs integrate skills with content and facilitate a deeper reading of texts.

The first step in teaching students to analyze and evaluate the different types of text is to get them used to asking *themselves* questions about the texts they read. Good readers are like good detectives: they ask questions, search for clues, make inferences, and use their own knowledge and experience to extract meaning from complex texts. They consider all of the evidence available to them while asking themselves important questions about the accuracy, validity, and reliability of each source. They understand that authors, like witnesses in a criminal investigation, sometimes contradict each other, not because they are necessarily dishonest (although that is sometimes the case), but because they are writing or speaking from their own point of view—a unique perspective shaped by a multitude of factors. In addition to not having all of the facts or otherwise lacking a clear understanding of the topic, authors' backgrounds—their socio-economic status, gender, occupation, religious beliefs and affiliations, political persuasion, national identity, prejudices, past experiences, and personal agendas—may influence what they do or do not say.

Questions Students Should Ask About Every Text

There are eight important questions students should ultimately ask themselves about *every* text they read: What type of text is this? Who is its author? When was it created? Why was it created? For whom was it created? What argument(s) does the author make? Is it believable? Why or why not? (see Figure 3.2). At first, we, as teachers, may want to write these questions on

Common Core Connection

ELA Literacy Standards for Informational Text

Grade 3
RI.3.1: Ask and answer questions to demonstrate understanding of a text, referring explicitly to the text as the basis for the answers.
RI.3.2: Determine the main idea of a text; recount the key details and explain how they support the main idea.
RI.3.4: Determine the meaning of general academic and domain-specific words and phrases in a text relevant to a grade 3 topic or subject area.
RI.3.6: Distinguish their own point of view from that of the author of a text.
RI.3.7: Use information gained from illustrations (e.g., maps, photographs) and the words in a text to demonstrate understanding of the text (e.g., where, when, why, and how key events occur).
RI.3.10: By the end of the year, read and comprehend informational texts, including history/social studies, science, and technical texts, at the high end of the grades 2–3 text complexity band independently and proficiently.

Grade 4
RI.4.1: Refer to details and examples in a text when explaining what the text says explicitly and when drawing inferences from a text.
RI.4.2: Determine the main idea of a text and explain how it is supported by key details; summarize the text.
RI.4.4: Determine the meaning of general academic and domain-specific words and phrases in a text relevant to a grade 4 topic or subject area.
RI.4.7: Interpret information presented visually, orally, or quantitatively (e.g., in charts, graphs, diagrams, time lines, animations, or interactive elements on Web pages) and explain how the information contributes to an understanding of the text in which it appears.
RI.4.8: Explain how an author uses reason and evidence to support particular points in a text.
RI.4.10: By the end of the year, read and comprehend informational texts, including history/social studies, science, and technical texts, in the grades 4–5 text complexity band proficiently, with scaffolding as needed at the high end of the range.

Grade 5
RI.5.1: Quote accurately from a text when explaining what the text says explicitly and when drawing inferences from the text.
RI.5.2: Determine two or more main ideas of a text and explain how they are supported by key details; summarize the text.
RI.5.4: Determine the meaning of general academic and domain-specific words and phrases in a text relevant to a grade 5 topic or subject area.
RI.5.8: Explain how an author uses reasons and evidence to support particular points in a text, identifying which reasons and evidence support which point(s).
RI.8.8: Delineate and evaluate the argument and specific claims in a text, assessing whether the reasoning is sound and the evidence is relevant and sufficient; recognize when irrelevant evidence is introduced.
RI.8.10: By the end of the year, read and comprehend literary nonfiction at the high end of the grades 6–8 text complexity band independently and proficiently.

Grade 9–10
RI.9–10.1: Cite strong and thorough textual evidence to support analysis of what the text says explicitly as well as inferences drawn from the text.
RI.9–10.2: Determine a central idea of a text and analyze its development over the course of the text, including how it emerges and is shaped and refined by specific details; provide an objective summary of the text.

Figure 3.1 Common Core Literacy Standards for Informational Text

Source: CCSSI, 2010

RI.9–10.3: Analyze how the author unfolds an analysis or series of ideas or events, including the order in which the points are made, how they are introduced and developed and the connections that are drawn between them.
RI.9–10.4: Determine the meaning of words and phrases as they are used in a text, including figurative, connotative, and technical meanings; analyze the cumulative impact of specific word choices on meaning and tone (e.g., how the language of a court opinion differs from that of a newspaper).
RI.9–10.6: Determine an author's point of view or purpose in a text and analyze how an author uses rhetoric to advance that point of view or purpose.
RI.9–10.8: Delineate and evaluate the argument and specific claims in a text, assessing whether the reasoning is valid and the evidence is relevant and sufficient; identify false statements and fallacious reasoning.
RI.9–10.9: Analyze seminal U.S. documents of historical and literary significance (e.g., Washington's Farewell Address, the Gettysburg Address, Roosevelt's Four Freedoms speech, King's "Letter from Birmingham Jail"), including how they address related themes and concepts.
RI.9–10.10: By the end of grade 10, read and comprehend literary nonfiction at the high end of the grades 9–10 text complexity band independently and proficiently.

Grades 11–12
RI.11–12.1: Cite strong and thorough textual evidence to support analysis of what the text says explicitly as well as inferences drawn from the text, including determining where the text leaves matters uncertain.
RI.11–12.2: Determine two or more central ideas of a text and analyze their development over the course of a text, including how they interact and build on one another to provide a complex analysis; provide an objective summary of the text.
RI.11–12.4: Determine the meaning of words and phrases as they are used in a text, including figurative, connotative, and technical meanings; analyze how an author uses and refines the meaning of a key term or terms over the course of a text (e.g., how Madison defines *faction* in *Federalist No. 10*).
RI.11–12.6: Determine an author's point of view or purpose in a text in which the rhetoric is particularly effective, analyzing how style and content contribute to the power, persuasiveness, or beauty of a text.
RI.11–12.8: Delineate and evaluate the reasoning in seminal U.S. texts, including the application of constitutional principles and use of legal reasoning (e.g., in U.S. Supreme Court majority opinions and dissents) and the premises, purposes, and arguments in works of public advocacy (e.g., *The Federalist*, presidential addresses).
RI.11–12.9: Analyze seventeenth, eighteenth, and nineteenth-century foundational U.S. documents of historical and literary significance (including the Declaration of Independence, the Preamble to the U.S. Constitution, the Bill of Rights, and Lincoln's Second Inaugural Address) for their themes, purposes, and rhetorical features.
RI.11–12.10: By the end of grade 12, read and comprehend literary nonfiction at the high end of the grades 11–CCR text complexity band independently and proficiently.

History/Social Studies Literacy Standards for Informational Text

Grades 6–8
RH.6–8.1: Cite specific textual evidence to support analysis of primary and secondary sources.
RH.6–8.2: Determine the central ideas or information of a primary or secondary source; provide an accurate summary of the source distinct from prior knowledge or opinions.
RH.6–8.4: Determine the meaning of words and phrases as they are used in a text, including vocabulary specific to domains related to history/social studies.
RH.6–8.6: Identify aspects of a text that reveal an author's point of view or purpose (e.g., loaded language, inclusion or avoidance of particular facts).
RH.6–8.8: Distinguish among fact, opinion, and reasoned judgment in a text.

Figure 3.1 *(Continued)*

RH.6–8.10: By the end of grade 8, read and comprehend history/social studies texts in the grades 6–8 text complexity band independently and proficiently.

Grades 9–10
RH.9–10.1: Cite specific textual evidence to support analysis of primary and secondary sources, attending to such features as the date and origin of the information.
RH.9–10.2: Determine the central ideas or information of a primary or secondary source; provide an accurate summary of how key events or ideas develop over the course of the text.
RH.9–10.4: Determine the meaning of words and phrases as they are used in a text, including vocabulary describing political, social, or economic aspects of history/social science.
RH.9–10.8: Assess the extent to which the reasoning and evidence in a text support the author's claims.
RH.9–10.10: By the end of grade 10, read and comprehend history/social studies texts in the grades 9–10 text complexity band independently and proficiently.

Grades 11–12
RH.11–12.1: Cite specific textual evidence to support analysis of primary and secondary sources, connecting insights gained from specific details to an understanding of the text as a whole.
RH.11–12.2: Determine the central ideas or information of a primary or secondary source; provide an accurate summary that makes clear the relationships among the key details and ideas.
RH.11–12.4: Determine the meaning of words and phrases as they are used in a text, including analyzing how an author uses and refines the meaning of a key term over the course of a text (e.g., how Madison defines *faction* in *Federalist* No. 10).
RH.11–12.8: Evaluate an author's premises, claims, and evidence by corroborating or challenging them with other information.
RH.11–12.10: By the end of grade 12, read and comprehend history/social studies texts in the grades 11–12 CCR text complexity band independently and proficiently.

Science and Technical Subjects Literacy Standards for Informational Text

Grades 6–8
RST.6–8.1: Cite specific textual evidence to support analysis of science and technical texts.
RST.6–8.2: Determine the central ideas or conclusions of a text; provide an accurate summary of the text distinct from prior knowledge or opinions.
RST.6–8.4: Determine the meaning of symbols, key terms, and other domain-specific words and phrases as they are used in a specific scientific or technical context relevant to grades 6–8 texts and topics.
RST.6–8.6: Analyze the author's purpose in providing an explanation, describing a procedure, or discussing an experiment in a text.
RST.6–8.8: Distinguish among facts, reasoned judgment based on research findings, and speculation in a text.
RST.6–8.10: By the end of grade 8, read and comprehend science/technical texts in the grades 6-8 text complexity band independently and proficiently.

Grades 9–10
RST.9–10.1: Cite specific textual evidence to support analysis of science and technical texts, attending to the precise details of explanations or descriptions.
RST.9–10.2: Determine the central ideas or conclusions of a text; trace the text's explanation or depiction of a process, phenomenon, or concept; provide an accurate summary of the text.
RST.9–10.4: Determine the meaning of symbols, key terms, and other domain-specific words and phrases as they are used in a specific scientific or technical context relevant to grades 9–10 texts and topics.
RST.9–10.6: Analyze the author's purpose in providing an explanation, describing a procedure, or discussing an experiment in a text, defining the question the author seeks to address.

Figure 3.1 *(Continued)*

RST.9–10.8: Assess the extent to which the reasoning and evidence in a text support the author's claim or a recommendation for solving a scientific or technical problem.
RST.9–10.10: By the end of grade 10, read and comprehend science/technical texts in the grades 9–10 text complexity band independently and proficiently.

Grades 11–12
RST.11–12.1: Cite specific textual evidence to support analysis of science and technical texts, attending to important distinctions the author makes to any gaps or inconsistencies in the account.
RST.11–12.2: Determine the central ideas or conclusions of a text; summarize complex concepts, processes, or information presented in a text by paraphrasing them in simpler but still accurate terms.
RST.11–12.4: Determine the meaning of symbols, key terms, and other domain-specific words and phrases as they are used in a specific scientific or technical context relevant to grades 11–12 texts and topics.
RST.11–12.6: Analyze the author's purpose in providing an explanation, describing a procedure, or discussing an experiment in a text, identifying important issues that remain unresolved.
RST.11–12.8: Evaluate the hypotheses, data, analysis, and conclusions in a science or technical text, verifying the data when possible and corroborating or challenging conclusions with other sources of information.
RST.11–12.10: By the end of grade 12, read and comprehend science/technical texts in the grades 11–CCR text complexity band independently and proficiently.

Figure 3.1 *(Continued)*

1. What type of text is this?
2. Who is its author?
3. When was it created?
4. Why was it created?
5. For whom was it created?
6. What argument(s) does the author make?
7. Is it believable?
8. Why or why not?

Figure 3.2 Eight Questions Students Should Ask About Every Text

the board or post them elsewhere in the classroom for easy reference. Over time, students will get used to posing them almost without thinking, regardless of the number or types of sources with which they are working. In the meantime, students need practice asking their *own* questions about different types of text, as this facilitates deeper reading and analytical thinking. Any text that captures students' interest and can generate meaningful discussion is a good one to start with. However, because many students find visual texts less intimidating—and more engaging—than word-based texts, I often have my own students practice asking questions about visual texts first.

Take, for example, Pieter Bruegel's 1562 painting, *The Triumph of Death* (see Figure 3.3). When we, as teachers, look at this painting, we can immediately tell that it depicts a scene that is frightening, gruesome, and chaotic. The landscape is desolate, fires burn in the distance, and corpses are everywhere. Those still alive appear to be engaged in a life-or-death struggle with an army of skeletons—a struggle they seem to be losing. As we study the painting more closely, we see skeletons hauling a cart full of skulls, a starving dog eating the flesh of a woman, a man whose head is about to be cut off by a skeleton brandishing a sword, and a skeleton on horseback killing people with a scythe. We see that people from all walks of life are represented—peasants, nobles, knights, churchmen—and that death does not discriminate between men and women or people of different classes.

Inevitably, we begin to ask ourselves questions about what we see in the painting: Who are these people? Why has death come for them? What does death represent? Is it possible that death represents some horrible outbreak of disease, like the plague, that ravaged Western Europe during the 16th century? Could it represent some other type of pestilence, like war or famine? Or could it represent the apocalypse? Is this a scene from a vision or dream the artist had,

Figure 3.3 *The Triumph of Death* by Pieter Bruegel

Source: Wikipedia

or is it an exaggeration of something calamitous that actually happened (and the artist himself personally witnessed)? These are the kinds of questions we want students to ask about this painting. However, students have a tendency, at least at first, to ask questions that are far more superficial. For example, students might ask: Why are there skeletons? Why are the skeletons killing people? Why is there a cart full of skulls? What's up with the dog (why is it there)? Why is there a skeleton on horseback? Why aren't the other skeletons riding horses? Why do the skeletons have different weapons? While there is nothing inherently wrong with asking these questions (after all, there are no *bad* questions here), these questions do not require any analytical thought. In these questions, students are simply regurgitating what they see in the painting.

Soliciting High-Order Questions from Students

We, as teachers, want students to move beyond asking questions like these and ask questions—like those in the previous paragraph—that require analytical thinking. For this reason, we can use the following strategy to solicit high-order questions from students:

- Project the painting onto a screen at the front of the classroom and have students study it silently for a minute.
- Ask students to describe the scene using a single word. (When I use Bruegel's painting in my global history classes, students often say things like "dark," "scary," "crazy," "sad," "chaotic," "death," "depressing," or "war.")
- Have students identify exactly what they see in the painting. What we want now is for students to provide us with specific details about the painting—textual evidence, if you will, that supports their one-word description of the scene as a whole. Write down what they say, either on the board or on a piece of paper large enough for everyone to see.
- Ask students to share any questions they have about what they see.

If students' questions seem superficial, we can probe them to get them to think more deeply about the painting. For example, if my students and I are looking at Bruegel's painting and one of them asks why there are skeletons, I will respond by asking him or her whether or not the skeletons could represent something. Invariably, the student will say something like "yeah, probably," in which case I will ask him or her to suggest a possibility. If his or her suggestion is off the mark, I may ask him or her another follow-up question in order to solicit a suggestion that seems more plausible. For example, if the student tells me that the skeletons might represent corpses (a suggestion I have gotten a couple of times), I will ask him or her to tell me what the skeletons are doing. When the student says "killing people," I will ask him or her to provide me with one or two things we have discussed in global history that killed large numbers of people. Without fail, the student will land on a correct response: war, disease, famine, or religious conflict.

Of course, the purpose of this exercise is not to seek answers to any of students' specific questions but to get them in the habit of asking themselves questions—*good* questions—about their reading. To illustrate how we can use the same strategy to facilitate a deeper reading of word-based text, I have used an excerpt from John S.C. Abbott's biography of Christopher Columbus (1877):

> Gradually Columbus came to the conclusion that the world must be a globe; and that, by sailing directly west, the shores of Asia would eventually be reached. By his measurement of the sun's apparent speed, he had formed a pretty accurate estimate of the size of the globe. It was not his supposition that there was any land between Europe and Asia on the west, but he expected that one would reach the coast of Asia about where he subsequently found the shores of the New World.
>
> *Source:* Abbott, J.S.C. (1877). *Christopher Columbus.* New York: Dodd, Mead, and Company.

Like Bruegel's *The Triumph of Death*, a careful reading of this passage will leave students with a number of good, high-order questions: How did Columbus know the world was round? Why was he so sure it wasn't flat? How was he able to use the Sun's "speed" to measure the circumference of the Earth? If he was able to figure out that the Earth was round, then why wasn't he able to figure out that the Earth was actually moving, and not the sun? If no one had ever sailed west across the Atlantic Ocean, how could he assume that there was no land between Europe and Asia? Wasn't he afraid?

Graphic Organizers for Practice

At first, it may be best to complete this exercise as a class. However, as students become more comfortable asking questions about their reading, they can begin to work more independently. If we want students to complete this exercise individually or as part of a small group, we can have them use a simple graphic organizer (see Figure 3.4) to record their questions. This exercise works very well for each of the nonfiction text types and can be used by teachers in all grades and content areas to get students asking good, high-order questions about their reading. Of course, there are literally hundreds of visual and nonvisual texts we could use for this exercise. A science teacher, for instance, could use a picture of the solar system to get students asking questions such as: Which way do the planets move? Are the years longer for planets that are far from the sun? Do the bigger planets have longer days? Do some planets orbit faster than others? Why are the planets different colors? What are the planets made of? Why do some have moons, while others don't? Why do some have rings? Is the sun another kind of planet? If the sun is a star, why is it bigger than other stars? Why do we get heat from it? A math teacher could use a photograph of a pyramid in Egypt to get students asking questions about geometry: Why did the Egyptians choose a pyramid shape? How did they know what angles to use? How did they know the pyramid wouldn't collapse? Why did they use a square pyramid instead of some other type of pyramid

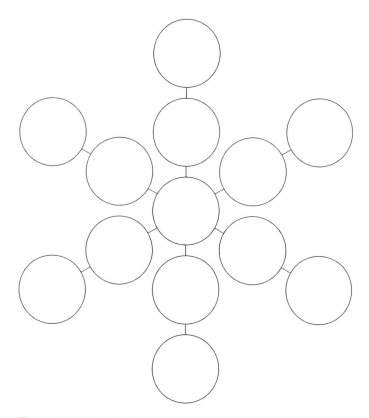

Figure 3.4 Graphic Organizer

(i.e. triangular)? Why did they use regular polygons as a base? How did they get the sides of the pyramid to meet perfectly in the center? Why did they use right pyramids instead of oblique pyramids? How big is the pyramid inside (how do you find its volume)? How do you find its surface area? A language arts teacher could use *Who Was Harriet Tubman?* (McDonough, 2002), a biography for third-grade readers, to get students asking questions about Tubman's life as a slave and her activities with the Underground Railroad: How were slaves kidnapped from Africa? Why were Africans the ones they kidnapped? Why did the northern states get rid of slavery, but not the South? Why did slaves have to live in small cabins? Why didn't they live in houses? Did all slaves run away the same way Harriet did? Why didn't Canada have slaves? Why were the slaves safe there? Why would Harriet stop being a conductor on the Underground Railroad just because slave owners wanted her dead? Couldn't she just keep hiding? If the slaves were set free, why couldn't they do everything white people could do? Why didn't Harriet ever learn to read and write?

The Questions Game

When I find that my students are struggling to come up with their own good, high-order questions about their reading, I sometimes use a variation of a strategy called the Questions Game to get their juices flowing. I first read about this strategy in Janet Allen's book *Reading History: A Practical Guide to Improving Literacy* (2005). According to Allen, this strategy was developed by Frank McTeague and was initially described in Aiden Chambers' book *Tell Me: Children, Reading, and Talk* (1996). In this exercise, students use the questions and insights offered by their peers to come up with more and better questions about their reading:

- First, have students study the assigned text silently for a few minutes.
- Then, ask them to write down at least three questions they have about their reading. Have students exchange questions with a partner and discuss possible answers to each other's questions.
- Once students have had a few minutes for discussion, tell them to come up with two or three new questions about their reading. These questions can be extensions of questions posed by their partners or new questions that came out of their discussion.
- Finally, have each pair of students exchange questions with another pair of students and repeat the process. Do this as many times as you feel will allow students to come up with more good, high-order questions about their reading.

This strategy is great because it can be used by teachers in all grades and content areas, works with visual and nonvisual texts, and can help struggling students generate their own good, high-order questions about the texts they read. When I use this strategy with my own students, I have them complete a graphic organizer similar to the one in Figure 3.4.

The SOAPSTone Technique

Once students have become accustomed to asking high-order questions about their reading, we, as teachers, need to help them organize their questions in a way that will enable them to extrapolate meaning from texts. The most effective strategy I use with my own students for this purpose is SOAPSTone (Speaker, Occasion, Audience, Purpose, Subject, and Tone), a technique originally conceived as a method for dissecting the work of professional writers (Morse, n.d.). I first learned about this technique when I attended AP training back in 2003. Today, however, I use it with all my students. Like the previous exercise, it works well for each of the nonfiction text types and can be used by teachers in all grades and content areas to get students asking the fundamental questions I identified and emphasized at the beginning of this chapter: Speaker (Who is the author?), Occasion (When was it created?), Audience (For whom was it created?), Purpose (Why was it created?), Subject (What argument does the author make?), and Tone (What is the author's attitude?). Students should attempt to answer these questions using evidence from the text and, based on their answers, determine whether or not the author's argument(s) is believable (see Figure 3.5).

Take, for example, a cigarette advertisement from 1930 (see Figure 3.6). In this case, the speaker (or author) is an organization rather than a single person, the American Tobacco Company. We know a little about its background: it was the manufacturer of Lucky Strike cigarettes during the 1930s (occasion). The audience, or the people for whom this ad was created, are

---

Speaker (Who is the author?)
Occasion (When was it created?)
Audience (For whom was it created?)
Purpose (Why was it created?)
Subject (What argument does the author make?)
Tone (What is the author's attitude?)
Is the author's argument believable? Why or why not?

Figure 3.5 SOAPSTone Technique for Analyzing Texts

Questions Students Should Be Asking

Figure 3.6 1930s "Lucky Strikes" Advertisement. The American Tobacco Company

Source: From the collection of Stanford University *(tobacco.stanford.edu<http://tobacco.stanford.edu>)*

consumers—people who currently smoke a brand of cigarettes other than Lucky Strike, people who smoke Lucky Strikes but are thinking about quitting or switching to another brand, and people who currently do not smoke but could be persuaded to start smoking. The purpose of the ad is to sell cigarettes—specifically, to convince consumers that Lucky Strikes can actually be good for their health. The subject (or argument) made by the manufacturer is that if so many doctors say smoking Luckies is okay, then they must be healthy. Evidence of this includes the 20,679 physicians who say that Luckies protect the throat against irritation and cough more than other cigarettes and the smiling, benevolent physician who is prescribing Luckies to his patients. We can infer that at least some of the doctors surveyed for this ad are smokers themselves and that those who do smoke prefer Lucky Strike to any other cigarette brand. Furthermore, these physicians may have been paid to participate in this survey and endorse Lucky Strikes. The tone (or attitude) of the manufacturer is warm, inviting, and reassuring. The American Tobacco Company wants to reassure consumers that Lucky Strikes are good for their overall health.

But is this ad believable? For someone living during the 1930s, maybe, given that people at that time knew far less than we do now about the dangers of cigarette smoking. Today, however, probably not, because we *do* know that smoking cigarettes—including Lucky Strikes—can lead to cancer, heart disease, and a variety of other health problems. Additionally, while many doctors during the 1930s endorsed Lucky Strikes, we do not know how many doctors refused to do so, either because Luckies were not more healthy than other cigarettes or because these doctors condemned smoking in general. Therefore, it is possible that the doctors who endorsed Lucky Strikes were very much a minority within the medical community.

The SOAPSTone technique is very effective for helping students learn how to analyze and evaluate visual and nonvisual texts. The following word-based example is an excerpt from a factory worker's complaints to the Factory Inquiry Commission in Great Britain about working conditions in 1833:

Ms. Hannah Goode: I work at Mr. Wilson's Mill. I think the youngest child is about 7. I daresay there are 20 under 9 years. It is about half past five by our clock at home when we go in . . . We come out at seven by the mill. We never stop to take our meals, except at dinner.

William Crookes is overlooker in our room. He is cross-tempered sometimes. He does not beat me; he beats the little children if they do not do their work right . . . I have sometimes seen the little children drop asleep or so, but not lately. If they are catched asleep, they get the strap. They are always very tired at night . . . I can read a little; I can't write. I used to go to school before I went to the mill.

Source: Hellerstein, E., Hume, L. & Offen, K. (Eds.) (1981). *A Documentary Account of Women's Lives in Nineteenth Century England, France, and the United States.* California: Stanford University Press.

Obviously, the speaker, or author of this text, is a factory worker named Hannah Goode. She is describing her working conditions to a parliamentary commission (audience) tasked with investigating working conditions. The occasion, or year in which the text was created, is 1833—the same year, incidentally, that laws were passed in Great Britain to limit the number of hours and types of jobs that women and children could work. The purpose of the text is to convince the commission that working conditions are poor, at least for Hannah and others working in her factory, perhaps in the hope that something will be done about it. The subject (argument) is that hours are long, breaks are few, and the children are mistreated. Also, Hannah has no time for school now that she works at the mill. She knows how to read a little only because she got to attend school before she started working. She is obviously disgruntled (tone) about the working conditions she and the other workers are made to endure.

However, while Hannah may be telling the whole truth about conditions in her factory, we, as readers, must consider the possibility that she is exaggerating in order to get sympathy from the members of the commission. On the other hand, if Hannah is afraid of reprisal from her employer, she may actually be leaving out more damning information in hopes that she will not get fired. Additionally, Hannah could not have written down her own testimony, as she stated in the text that she could read a little but could not write. Therefore, the person who wrote her testimony down on paper for her (a friend, commissioner, or fellow worker) may have added, omitted, or otherwise changed her actual testimony in order to make conditions sound better or worse than they actually were.

At first, it may be best for students to practice using the SOAPSTone technique as part of class discussion. However, as they begin to feel more comfortable with this technique, they can start to use it on their own (see Figure 3.7). For instance, a U.S. Government teacher could have students use SOAPSTone to analyze and evaluate presidential campaign commercials; a language arts teacher could have students use it to analyze magazine, newspaper, or TV advertisements and identify logical fallacies. A science teacher could have students use this technique to analyze and evaluate an article written by an environmentalist group about the dangers of global warming; a math teacher could use it to teach his or her students how to use language to work through word problems. Of course, these are just a few ideas; the possibilities are endless. Whatever the subject, whatever students' grade level, the SOAPSTone technique is an effective strategy for helping students learn how to organize their own questions about their reading and use those questions to analyze and evaluate a wide variety of nonfiction texts.

```
SPEAKER (Who is the author?):
_____
_____

OCCASION (When was it created?):
_____
_____

AUDIENCE (For whom was it created?):
_____
_____

PURPOSE (Why was it created?):
_____
_____

SUBJECT (What argument does the author make?):
_____
_____

Evidence author uses to support argument:
_____

Evidence author uses to support argument:
_____

Evidence author uses to support argument:
_____

TONE (What is the author's attitude?):
_____

Is the author's argument believable?      YES      NO
Why or Why not?:
_____
_____
_____
_____
```

Figure 3.7 Handout: Analyzing Texts Using the SOAPSTone Technique

Summary

The first step in teaching students to analyze and evaluate the different types of nonfiction text is to get them used to asking *themselves* questions about the texts they read. There are several effective strategies we can use to get students in the habit of asking these kinds of questions about their reading. Once students have become accustomed to asking these kinds of questions, we can use the SOAPSTone technique to help them organize their questions in a way that will allow them to extrapolate meaning from complex texts. Like the other strategies presented in this chapter, the SOAPSTone technique works well for each of the nonfiction text types and can be used by teachers in all grades and content areas to get students asking those eight all-important questions I emphasized in this chapter.

At first, it may be best to implement each of the strategies presented in this chapter during class discussions. However, as students become more comfortable asking questions about their reading, they can begin to work more independently. We can use graphic organizers to help students generate their own good, high-order questions about their reading and use the SOAPSTone technique to organize those questions independently (or as part of a small group).

How might you get your students asking good, high-order questions about their reading? Feel free to write some of your own ideas here:

_____
_____
_____
_____
_____
_____
_____
_____
_____
_____

References

Abbott, J.S.C. (1877). *Christopher Columbus.* New York: Dodd, Mead, and Company.

Allen, J. (2005). *Reading History: A Practical Guide to Improving Literacy.* Oxford: Oxford University Press.

Chambers, A. (1996). *Tell Me: Children, Reading, and Talk.* Portland: Stenhouse.

Common Core State Standards Initiative (CCSSI). (2010, June). *Common Core State Standards for English Language Arts & Literacy in the History/Social Studies, Science, and Technical Subjects.* Retrieved from www.corestandards.org/ELA-Literacy

Hellerstein, E., Hume, L., & Offen, K. (Eds.) (1981). *A Documentary Account of Women's Lives in Nineteenth Century England, France, and the United States.* California: Stanford University Press.

McDonough, Y.Z. (2002). *Who Was Harriet Tubman?* New York: Grosset & Dunlap.

Morse, O. (n.d.). *SOAPSTone: A Strategy for Reading and Writing.* Princeton: The College Board. Retrieved from http://apcentral.collegeboard.com/apc/public/preap/teachers_corner/45200.html

CHAPTER

Working With Multiple Texts

Once students become comfortable analyzing individual texts, we, as teachers, need to show them how to work with multiple texts. After all, most of the work people do, both in college and on the job, requires them to analyze and evaluate multiple texts. Students in college, for instance, have to analyze and evaluate any number of visual and nonvisual texts (including primary and secondary sources) in order to write required research papers. In the business world, employees have to analyze and evaluate data presented in a variety of different formats, including written reports, pie charts, bar graphs, spreadsheets, and databases in order to prepare their own reports, proposals, or presentations. Therefore, students need to learn how to synthesize information in addition to analyzing and evaluating individual texts. Specifically, they need to understand the relationship between texts and how they work together to answer a question or solve a problem. They need to be able to compare texts to one another and understand how one text fills in gaps left by another text. They need to know how to integrate background knowledge with knowledge they have gleaned from a text and recognize what perspective(s) or types of text are missing and would be helpful. Finally, students need to be able to formulate an argument, or thesis statement, in response to text-based questions and support their thesis with evidence from each one of the texts.

So crucial are these skills to college and career readiness in the 21st century that their mastery is required by the Common Core State Standards. For instance, the Common Core anchor standards for reading state that students must be able to integrate and evaluate content presented in diverse media and formats and analyze how two or more texts address similar themes or topics in order to build knowledge. By the time they reach high school, the Standards say that students should be proficient at synthesizing information from multiple sources and be able to cite evidence from them in order to support an argument. Like the reading standards, the anchor standards for writing emphasize analytical reasoning and require that students use "relevant and sufficient evidence to support claims in an analysis of substantive topics or texts." Students are to "gather relevant information from multiple print and digital sources, assess the credibility and accuracy of each source, and integrate the information" in order to build knowledge (CCSSI, 2010). The literacy standards for social studies, science, and technical subjects use similar language to emphasize the importance of learning how to analyze and evaluate information from multiple sources (see Figure 4.1).

Common Core Connection

ELA Literacy Standards for Informational Text

Grade 3
RI.3.9: Compare and contrast the most important points and key details presented in two texts on the same topic.

Grade 4
RI.4.6: Compare and contrast a first-hand and second-hand account of the same event or topic; describe the differences in focus and the information provided.
RI.4.9: Integrate information from two texts on the same topic in order to write or speak about the subject knowledgeably.

Grade 5
RI.5.6: Analyze multiple accounts of the same event or topic, noting important similarities and differences in the point of view they represent.
RI.5.7: Draw on information from multiple print or digital sources, demonstrating the ability to locate an answer to a question quickly or solve a problem efficiently.
RI.5.9: Integrate information from several texts on the same topic in order to write or speak about the subject knowledgeably.

Grade 6
RI.6.7: Integrate information presented in different media or formats (e.g., visually, quantitatively) as well as in words to develop a coherent understanding of a topic or issue.
RI.6.9: Compare and contrast one author's presentation of events with that of another (e.g., a memoir written by and a biography on the same person).

Grade 7
RI.7.7: Compare and contrast a text to an audio, video, or multimedia version of the text, analyzing each medium's portrayal of the subject (e.g., how the delivery of speech affects the impact of words).
RI.7.9: Analyze how two or more authors writing about the same topic shape their presentations of key information by emphasizing different evidence or advancing different interpretations of facts.

Grade 8
RI.8.7: Evaluate the advantages and disadvantages of using different mediums (e.g., print or digital text, video, multimedia) to present a particular topic or idea.
RI.8.9: Analyze a case in which two or more texts provide conflicting information on the same topic and identify where the texts disagree on matters of fact or interpretation.

Grades 9–10
RI.9–10.7: Analyze various accounts of a subject told in different mediums (e.g., a person's life story in both print and multimedia), determining which details are emphasized in each account.

Figure 4.1 Common Core Literacy Standards for Multiple Texts
Source: CCSSI, 2010

Grades 11–12
RI.11–12.7: Integrate and evaluate multiple sources of information presented in different media and formats (e.g., visually, quantitatively) as well as in words in order to address a question or solve a problem.

History/Social Studies Literacy Standards for Informational Text

Grades 6–8
RH.6–8.7: Integrate visual information (e.g., in charts, graphs, photographs, videos, or maps) with other information in print and digital texts.
RH.6–8.9: Analyze the relationship between a primary and secondary source on the same topic.

Grades 9–10
RH.9–10.6: Compare the point of view of two or more authors for how they treat the same or similar topics, including which details they include and emphasize in their respective accounts.
RH.9–10.7: Integrate quantitative or technical analysis (e.g., charts, research data) with qualitative analysis in print and digital texts.
RH.9–10.9: Compare and contrast treatments of the same topic in several primary and secondary sources.

Grades 11–12
RH.11–12.6: Evaluate authors' differing points of view on the same historical event or issue by assessing the authors' claims, reasoning, and evidence.
RH.11–12.7: Integrate and evaluate multiple sources of information presented in diverse media and formats (e.g., visually, quantitatively, as well as in words) in order to address a question or solve a problem.
RH.11–12.9: Integrate information from diverse sources, both primary and secondary, into a coherent understanding of an idea or event, noting discrepancies among sources.

Science and Technical Subjects Literacy Standards for Informational Text

Grades 6–8
RST.6–8.7: Integrate quantitative or technical information expressed in words in a text with a version of that information expressed visually (e.g., in a flowchart, diagram, model, graph, or table).
RST.6–8.9: Compare and contrast the information gained from experiments, simulations, video, or multimedia sources with that gained from reading a text on the same topic.

Grades 9–10
RST.9–10.9: Compare and contrast the findings presented in a text to those from other sources (including their own experiments) noting when the findings support or contradict previous explanations or accounts.

Grades 11–12
RST.11–12.7: Integrate and evaluate multiple sources of information presented in diverse formats and media (e.g., quantitative data, video, multimedia) in order to address a question or solve a problem.
RST.11–12.8: Evaluate the hypotheses, data, analysis, and conclusions in a science or technical text, verifying the data when possible and corroborating or challenging conclusions with other sources of information.
RST.11–12.9: Synthesize information from a range of sources (e.g., texts, experiments, simulations) into a coherent understanding of a process, phenomenon, or concept, resolving conflicting information when possible.

Figure 4.1 (*Continued*)

For this reason, it is imperative that we give our students practice working with multiple sources once we feel they have mastered the ability to analyze and evaluate individual texts (visual and nonvisual, primary and secondary). However, because students usually find visual texts less intimidating—and more engaging—than word-based text, I often have my own students work with visual texts first.

Getting Students to Think Critically About the Relationship Between Texts

We can use the following strategy to get students thinking critically about the relationship between texts and how they can work together to answer a question or solve a problem. This strategy helps put students at ease with analyzing multiple *visual* texts, works on developing several literacy skills at once, and is both simple and effective. It can be used by teachers in every grade and content area and be modified to reinforce any topic or concept students are studying during the year:

- Have students clear their desks of everything but a piece of paper and a writing utensil.
- Project a series of related visuals, one at a time, onto a screen.
- As you move through the slides, have students identify each visual on their own piece of paper.
- After you have shown them all of the slides, have students tell you what they wrote down for each visual.
- Once you have gone back through all of the visuals with the class in order to make sure students have the correct answers, ask students to tell you what all of the visuals have in common (or what they all describe).
- Then ask your students, "If these visuals could be used together to answer a question, what kind of question do you think we would be asked to answer about them?" (Teachers with very young students might choose to skip this step or approach it differently.)
- After you have solicited a number of good responses from your students, ask them to tell you what is missing from the visuals. This is the additional text that you want students to suggest—a visual that could be added to the list in order to help them more completely answer the question.
- Finally, ask students to group the visuals in as many appropriate ways as possible.

For example, we could ask elementary students to identify the image of a dog, cat, cow, and pig. Then, we could put the four images side by side and ask students to tell us what all of these animals have in common. Even at the elementary level, students should recognize that all four animals are mammals and that all four have been domesticated. Next, we could ask students to identify any differences they see between these animals. Are there traits common to two of these animals, for instance, but not the others? With some probing, students should be able to tell us that pigs and cows are animals that one would find on a farm, while dogs and cats are animals that people keep in their homes. Cows and pigs have hooves, while dogs and cats do not. Cats and dogs are trainable, while cows and pigs generally are not. Of course, students may come up with additional similarities or differences for these animals. Finally, we could ask students to tell us what other animals are like cows and pigs and what other animals are like dogs and cats.

If we were teaching a middle school science class, we could make this exercise more challenging by increasing the number of animals that students have to classify. For example, we could ask students to identify a frog, alligator, snake, salamander, horse, dolphin, duck, and penguin. When we ask students to group the visuals, students should recognize that all represent living things belonging to the animal kingdom; that the frog and salamander are both amphibians, the alligator and snake both reptiles, the horse and dolphin both mammals, the duck and penguin both birds; that some of these animals live on land and others live in the water; that some lay eggs while others give birth to live young; that some are warm-blooded and some are cold-blooded; that some stay with their young after they are born while others do not; and so on. The groupings are seemingly endless. That's great, because every time students come up with a new grouping, they are connecting insights gained from each one of the visuals individually to their understanding of the visuals as a whole. Finally, we could ask students to identify an animal, not depicted in any of the visuals, that belongs in one or more of the groups.

In my own classes, I employ this strategy many times during the year—when my students are studying river-valley civilizations; classical civilizations in Rome, China, and India; feudalism in medieval Europe and Japan; trade networks in Africa and Asia; the Scientific Revolution; and so on. When I use this exercise during their study of river-valley civilizations, for example, my students recognize that the visuals in the PowerPoint slides I show them—the Great Pyramids at Giza, an Egyptian calendar, several hieroglyphic writing tablets, a wagon wheel from Mesopotamia, a potter's wheel from India, a bronze bell from China, and a ziggurat from Mesopotamia, to name a few—all depict achievements made by early Mesopotamian, Egyptian, Indian, and Chinese civilizations. When I ask students to tell me what kind of question(s) they might be asked about these visuals collectively, they invariably offer up responses such as "Identify the different achievements made by ancient river-valley civilizations" or "What are the different achievements made by river-valley civilizations?" When I ask them to group the visuals, they are able to tell me that some of the visuals reflect achievements in monumental building, while others reflect achievements in (hieroglyphic) writing. Of course, as with the previous example, there are a number of different possible groupings. Finally, students are able to provide me with a number of additional achievements made by river-valley civilizations that are not depicted in any of the visuals. Pictures of these achievements, they say, would be helpful for answering the text-based question "What are the different achievements made by river-valley civilizations?" more completely.

At first, it may be best to complete this exercise as a class. However, as students become more comfortable thinking critically about the relationship between two or more visual texts, we can have them complete this exercise individually. Usually, I print my PowerPoint slides out as a handout for this purpose—making sure, of course, that I have numbered each one of the slides beforehand.

This strategy is great for helping students understand the relationship between two or more texts. Specifically, it helps students understand how different texts can work together to answer a question—a question they themselves craft after looking at each one of the visuals and thinking about how they relate to one another. It also helps them to think about what is missing from the texts and requires them to make use of any background information they have about the topic. It is less threatening than doing history, or science, or whatever subject(s) we teach, even though the texts—or visuals—themselves are all related to topics students have studied (or are studying) in our classes.

Making Text-Based Questions Fun for Students

Text-based questions are also less intimidating if they are about fun and interesting topics outside of the curriculum—like favorite teachers, school events, community athletics, or national celebrities. This is especially true of TBQs that require students to work with multiple *nonvisual* sources because nonvisual sources are sometimes less engaging—and more intimidating—for students than visual sources. Therefore, we can get students thinking critically about the relationship between two or more nonvisual texts by having them answer questions about things with which they are already familiar (and very comfortable). For example, I created the following TBQ to put my students at ease with analyzing nonvisual texts, get them thinking about the relationship between texts, and give them practice evaluating sources. My students really enjoy this TBQ because it is about a topic of interest that is familiar to them.

Text-Based Question

Using the following texts, analyze students' attitudes about Mr. Smith as a high school social studies teacher. Are there any additional texts you would like to see that might help you further analyze students' attitudes about Mr. Smith between 2003 and 2010?

Text #1

Adam Albright	3
Brian Baker	3
Christina Coker	3
John Doe	2
Elmo Eckerdt	3
Francesca Follows	4
Griswold Great	3
Heathcliff Harper	4
Jackie Juniper	4
Keith Kline	3
Larry Lake	3
Meredith Manners	3
Nadine Naples	3
Orlando Ondish	5
Peter Pestilence	3
Randy Restful	5
Steven Snod	2
Travis Turner	2

*3 or better constitutes a passing score
Percent passing: 83%
National passing rate: 51%

Source: Students' AP exam scores* in World History; Teacher: K. Smith; School: Florence Nightingale High.

Text #2

5/31/09: "Mr. Smith is by far the best teacher I've ever had. He gives a LOT of homework and his class is very time consuming, but you will learn a ton."
2/22/08: "Mr. Smith is probably the coolest teacher at the school. He's brilliant, and he knows just about everything that has ever happened in the history of the world. He's pretty funny too. His stories and his jokes go a long way to making the class fun and interesting."
4/29/07" "Mr. Smith is an exceptional teacher. He's a great lecturer and can answer almost any question you ask him. I would highly recommend him to anyone!"
5/11/06: "Mr. Smith is a caring guy and a pretty awesome teacher. I just wish he gave less homework."
6/05/04: "Yo, Mr. Smitty! I love you and all your cool stories, but take it easy on the homework!"

Source: Comments about Mr. Smith made on *tellusaboutyourfnhteacher.com*, a community website where students, parents, and other stakeholders can anonymously post their thoughts about teachers at Florence Nightingale High.

Text #3

Dear Mr. Smith,
I honestly cannot believe I am still alive after taking your class! Your class has been so stressful for me! I can't tell you how many hours I spent reading and outlining my textbook this year. It was exhausting! I went through so much notebook paper that I think I killed off an entire rainforest. Sometimes, I was so stressed out, I just had to cry. I remember forgetting to do my study guide one night. When I got to school the next morning and realized that I had forgotten it, I started bawling. My friends—the ones that didn't have you for a teacher—thought that I had totally lost it. They said, "Don't sweat it, Megan. What's the big deal?" I looked at them like they were crazy. "Oh, my God!" I told them. "You guys don't understand! Not having this study guide today is like the world coming to an end!"

Source: Excerpt from a letter written by Megan Turner, a former 10th-grade student, June 2008.

Text #4

I think what I loved most about you was your passion for history, and I know that I will never forget you. If you want, you can tell your students I said they should do your work and listen because it will truly pay off for them. As much as I hated working so hard in your class—reading and outlining the textbook, writing essays, completing projects, and taking killer tests—I am a much better student now because of it. Thanks so much for everything you did.

Source: Excerpt from a letter written by Rheanna Jenkins, a former 10th-grade student, 2008.

Text #5

Mr. Smith,
I just wanted to say thank you for being such a great teacher. The stuff I learned in World History my sophomore year and AP European History my senior year has really come in handy now that I'm in college. We talked about Locke this semester in philosophy, the Belle Epoch in French, and colonization in geography. I never realized how everything we learned ties into everything! I'll tell you what, though. I'm so glad I don't have to get up at six every morning for high school anymore. These days I can hardly manage to get out of bed at nine!

Hope you can love this year's students as much as you loved us!
Julia

Source: Email from Julia Manning, a former AP student, 2008.

Text #6

I hated Mr. Smith's class. He was a terrible teacher. All he did was talk about his stupid lady friends. I didn't want to hear about all the ugly women he dated! He gave too much work, his jokes were corny, and his classroom smelled like a dusty library. And those TBQs he made us do! They were awful. I think I failed every one of those stupid things. I can't believe I made a "D" in the class the second semester. I should have gotten at least a B! I wouldn't recommend him to anyone. Ugh! Not ever!

Source: Conversation between John Doe, a 10th-grade student, and some of his friends, Spring 2006.

Text #7

You've probably heard a lot of rumors about this class: Four hours of homework a night, 10 essays to write in one weekend, etcetera. However, while it is true that you will work very hard this semester, I can promise you that you will not have four hours of homework a night or have to write 10 essays in a single weekend—though you will write more than 10 essays over the course of the entire semester. The truth is that you can expect to have about 45 minutes of homework a night—some nights more, of course, and some nights less; and, every once in a while, you won't have any homework at all . . . And, of course, you'll get to hear great stories about some of my lady friends.

Source: Mr. Smith's address to his AP U.S. Government and Politics class, Day One, Spring 2010.

Text #8

11/2009: "You should give less busy-work and homework."
11/2009: "I haven't really learned anything in this class. Taking notes and creating the PowerPoint presentations leaves me to teach myself. Anything I have learned in this class I've taught to myself."
4/2008: "The room has no color. It's weird."
11/2007: "You should put yourself on a more personal level with students."
5/2006: "The tests are hard and I don't like the TBQs. Oh, and no more homework, please."

Source: Excerpts from students' evaluations of Mr. Smith, anonymous.

Text #9

5/2009: "Honestly, you are the best teacher I've ever had. You know what you're talking about and really care about seeing us be successful, which is really nice to know."
5/2008: "I love the class and I'm learning a lot. The teacher's organization helps me because I know exactly what is expected. I would love to take AP European History [with you] next year."
11/2005: "I really enjoy this class, all of the work is truly beneficial and you are always so willing to answer any of our questions."
5/2005: "You rock, Mr. Smith!"

> 5/2004: "Have a good summer with those lady friends. You're doing a great job! Keep it up! . . . The notes helped but sometimes just seemed like so much! But your class is great!"
>
> Source: Excerpts from students' evaluations of Mr. Smith, anonymous.

Using the SOAPSTone Technique to Analyze Multiple Texts

Rather than have students read all of these texts at once, we should have them move through the TBQ one text at a time. We can have students use the SOAPSTone technique to analyze each one of the texts individually, just as we did in the previous chapter. Then, students can connect the insights they gained from each one of the texts individually to their understanding of the texts as a whole. When working with multiple texts, we can use a handout like the one in Figure 4.2 to help students organize their thoughts. First, we should have students underline or circle important words and phrases in the question itself (assuming, of course, that we have asked students to write down the question or have printed the TBQ out for them). Since students are being asked to analyze students' attitudes about Mr. Smith as a high school social studies teacher, the following phrases are important to circle: "students' attitudes," "Mr. Smith," "social studies teacher." Students should also identify the date or time period the question includes (2003–2010) and circle the words "additional texts," since their response to the question will not be complete until they have suggested an additional type of source that helps further their analysis.

Second, we should ask our students to identify any words or phrases in the question that they need to have defined. The word "analysis," for instance, is one students might mention. Then, we should tap into students' background knowledge by asking them to share any words, phrases, or ideas that came to mind as soon as they read the question. Students may say things like "Most teachers have some students who like them and some who don't" and "Students who made an 'A' in his class probably think he's a good teacher, while students who made an 'F' in his class probably think he's a bad teacher." Tapping into students' background knowledge allows us to show students that they know more about the topic than they might otherwise think, and that they can actually predict, at least in some instances, what the sources themselves will say.

Once students have completed each of these steps, they can turn to the sources themselves—analyzing each one carefully, with the help of their teacher, one text at a time. Observant students may point out that text #1 offers little insight into students' attitudes about Mr. Smith, but helps put students' comments about him—positive or negative—into perspective. If 83 percent of his class passed the AP world history exam, they might say, he must be fairly effective, regardless of what students say about him. However, they may also point out that the text only includes results from the 2004 exam and that Mr. Smith's test results may not always have been so stellar. Therefore, access to additional score reports would be helpful.

After analyzing all of the texts, students should recognize that Mr. Smith's pupils gave him mixed reviews. Many students, of course, spoke very highly of him. They appreciated his passion for history and believed he had prepared them well for their end-of-course assessments and for other classes they would take in high school and in college. A few students, however, found his jokes corny, his stories distracting, and his methods ineffective. They said that he needed to put himself on a more personal level with students, give less busy work, and lower his expectations for performance. In fact, these students were so disgruntled that they began to spread rumors about his classes, telling incoming students that they would have four hours of homework a night and have to write 10 essays in a single weekend. Of course, many students will point out that the pupil speaking in text #6 seems resentful of his "D" and that other students who speak poorly of Mr. Smith might have earned low grades in his class as well. On the other hand, students who gave him positive reviews on evaluations conducted in the middle of the school year (see text #9) may have been afraid to criticize him if they suspected he might recognize their handwriting.

These are just a few of the observations students are likely to make when analyzing these texts using the SOAPSTone technique demonstrated in Chapter 3. Obviously, the objective of this exercise is to get students thinking critically about the relationship between nonvisual texts and to give them practice evaluating sources. Even though this TBQ is not related to any of the topics students will study in their classes, it is a great way to acclimate students to working with multiple texts because it is about a fun and interesting topic familiar to them.

Another TBQ I have used with my classes during the past 10 years is one about high school football. This TBQ was created by Larry Treadwell, a teacher in southern Florida.

Background Information

The annual Ely Tigers versus Dillard Panthers football game was played Friday night. Due to family commitments, my friend, who is a teacher at Ely High School, was unable to attend the game. The game was decided when Donnell

Wilson caught a touchdown pass on the last play of the fourth quarter, giving Ely a 14–10 victory. When he arrived at school Monday morning, everyone was talking about the "catch" and the victory. What my friend wants to know is what *really* happened and just how great of a play this catch actually was. Throughout the day, he spoke to the following people in an attempt to obtain the truth. He has asked us to help him by reviewing his report.

Text-Based Questions

What really happened at the Ely–Dillard football game? How great was Donnell's game-winning catch?

Text #1

The annual Ely–Dillard football game ended in a dramatic fashion when Donnell Wilson caught the game-winning touchdown pass as time expired. Wilson made a leaping catch and landed safely in the end zone, capping an improbable come-from-behind win for the Tigers.

(Note: Most high school game results are phoned in to the newspaper sports desk.)

Source: Tom Robard. Newspaper reporter for the *Fort Lauderdale Sun-Sentinel*.

Text #2

Did you see that catch? I mean, it was great! Man, I knew I had it! That D-back was nothing! I ran right by him and just reached out and pulled it in. Focus, real focus! We're number one!

Source: Donnell Wilson, Ely wide receiver who caught the winning pass.

Text #3

Great catch! Unbelievable! Donnell has heart and no quit in him. When it mattered, I knew he would come through. He's tough, a real gamer! I had the team focused. We were ready to play. Never a doubt!

Source: Clayton Sheffield, offensive coach for Ely High School.

Working With Multiple Texts

Text #4

It was a totally awesome catch! We won the game and, like, totally disgraced that other team! I knew we would win after our half-time show, and we did! We rock! Go Ely! Those Dillard guys had no chance. And you should have seen those Dillard girls! Their cheers were sloppy and screechy! No wonder we won!

Source: Jasmine McNeil, Ely cheerleader captain.

Text #5

Ely played real hard. Those boys were great. It was a great catch that won a hard-fought game. The noise in the stands after the game was unbelievable. Everyone was hugging each other and screaming.

Source: Mary Griffin, Ely teacher who attend the game to watch her son play.

Text #6

We were robbed. That guy never caught the ball. He was lying there on the ground and the ball fell in his hands. He pushed me, and the ref never saw nothing. Ely is nothing but a bunch of cheats!

Source: Demetrius Johnson, D-back who covered Donnell, Dillard High School.

Text #7

Demetrius played him real tight. Ely ended up on the ground with the ball and the touchdown. Some nights you just aren't lucky; some nights you are.

Source: Mark Burton, defensive coach, Dillard High School.

Text #8

It was a clean and simple catch, resulting in a touchdown. No penalty was involved.

Source: Owen Dyson, football referee. Excerpt from his game report to the Florida High School Athletic Association.

> **Text #9**
>
> #83 Donnell Wilson, Senior: Position: Wide Receiver
> Height: 5'6"
> Weight: 155
> Comment: Has only poor hands and average speed.
>
> *Source:* Robert Benson, assistant football coach for the University of Nebraska. Excerpt from his scouting report.

Like the TBQ I have students complete about me as a social studies teacher, this TBQ is about a topic of great interest to students. My students really enjoy analyzing each one of these texts and are able to point out important inconsistencies between the testimonies of coaches, parents, players, and other stakeholders interviewed by my "friend" at Ely High School. For instance, students always point out that Tom Robard, the newspaper reporter, said Donnell made a "leaping catch" and "landed safely in the end zone," while Donnell himself said he "simply reached out and pulled [the ball] in." They also point out that at least two people from the opposing team, a coach and a player, suggested that Donnell did not catch the ball at all. According to Demetrius Johnson, the Defensive-Back who covered Donnell during the game, the ball fell into Donnell's hands while he was "lying on the ground." Mark Burton, the defensive coach for Dillard High School, implied the same when he said that Donnell "ended up on the ground with the ball and the touchdown." Furthermore, students say that at least one expert about football, a scout from the University of Nebraska, implied that Donnell was not an exceptional player. The scout's comment that Donnell "has only poor hands and average speed" seems to support something Donnell's offensive coach said in text #3 about Donnell only coming through "when it mattered."

Of course, students recognize that each of the individuals interviewed in this TBQ are looking at the "catch" from their own point of view, and that a few of them may not have actually seen it. The cheerleading captain, for instance, may have been facing the stands and cheering at the time the catch was made, as she says nothing about the catch itself other than that it was "totally awesome." Mary Griffin, the mother of one of Donnell's teammates, also says little about the catch itself and may have been busy socializing in the stands when Donnell landed, reached out, or fell during the last few moments of the game.

Last, but not least, students say that additional texts would be helpful for determining what really happened at the Ely–Dillard football game. These include a video of the game as well as testimony from some of Donnell's teammates. Some students suggest that we interview the announcer at the game as well, as he would have surely seen the play and had a bird's eye view of the field from the press box.

Again, we can use a handout like the one in Figure 4.2 to help students organize their thoughts. At first, it may be best to complete this exercise as a class. However, as students become more comfortable using the SOAPSTone technique to analyze multiple texts, we can have them work more independently. Figure 4.2 is great to use for class discussions as well as for individual and small group practice.

TBQ—Multiple Text Analysis Worksheet: SOAPSTone Technique

1. Underline or circle important words or phrases in the question.
2. Are there any words or phrases in the question that you need to have defined for you? If so, write them here:
   _____
   _____
   _____

3. What do you already know about this topic?
   _____
   _____
   _____

4. Analyze each of one of the texts carefully using the SOAPSTone technique.

Text #1:

Speaker:_____
Occasion:_____
Audience:_____
Purpose:_____
Subject:_____
    Evidence #1:_____
    Evidence #2:_____
Tone:_____
Is it believable? Y/N Why or why not? _____

Text #2:

Speaker:_____
Occasion:_____
Audience:_____
Purpose:_____
Subject:_____
    Evidence #1:_____
    Evidence #2:_____
Tone:_____
Is it believable? Y/N Why or why not? _____

Figure 4.2 Multiple Text Analysis Worksheet: SOAPSTone Technique

Text #3:

Speaker: _____
Occasion: _____
Audience: _____
Purpose: _____
Subject: _____

    Evidence #1: _____
    Evidence #2: _____

Tone: _____
Is it believable? Y/N Why or why not? _____

Text #4:

Speaker: _____
Occasion: _____
Audience: _____
Purpose: _____
Subject: _____

    Evidence #1: _____
    Evidence #2: _____

Tone: _____
Is it believable? Y/N Why or why not? _____

Text #5:

Speaker: _____
Occasion: _____
Audience: _____
Purpose: _____
Subject: _____

    Evidence #1: _____
    Evidence #2: _____

Tone: _____
Is it believable? Y/N Why or why not? _____

Text #6:

Speaker: _____
Occasion: _____
Audience: _____
Purpose: _____
Subject: _____

    Evidence #1: _____
    Evidence #2: _____

Tone: _____
Is it believable? Y/N Why or why not? _____

Text #7:

Speaker: _____
Occasion: _____

Figure 4.2 (*Continued*)

Working With Multiple Texts

```
Audience:_____
Purpose:_____
Subject:_____
    Evidence #1:_____
    Evidence #2:_____
Tone:_____
Is it believable? Y/N  Why or why not? _____
```

Text #8:

```
Speaker:_____
Occasion:_____
Audience:_____
Purpose:_____
Subject:_____
    Evidence #1:_____
    Evidence #2:_____
Tone:_____
Is it believable? Y/N  Why or why not? _____
```

Text #9:

```
Speaker:_____
Occasion:_____
Audience:_____
Purpose:_____
Subject:_____
    Evidence #1:_____
    Evidence #2:_____
Tone:_____
Is it believable? Y/N  Why or why not? _____
```

5. Now, group the texts in as many appropriate ways as possible.

Texts _____ because _____
Texts _____ because _____
Texts _____ because _____
Texts _____ because _____

6. Finally, what other text(s) would you find helpful for answering this question? Write your response here:
_____
_____

Figure 4.2 (*Continued*)

While both of the TBQs I have used to illustrate this strategy consist of nine texts, TBQs can consist of any number of visual or nonvisual sources (or some combination of the two). If we feel that working with eight, nine, or ten texts at a time would be overwhelming for our students, we can start off by having them work with only two texts at once. Then, when they are ready, we can have them move on to analyzing three or more sources. However, my experience has been that once students master the ability to analyze individual texts using the SOAPSTone technique, they are able to handle working with more than five sources simultaneously. Of course, depending on our students and the nature of the question, fewer than five sources may be appropriate or necessary. That being the case, let's take a look at comparing two sources.

Comparing Two Texts Using the SOAPSTone Technique

As you probably guessed, our students will use the SOAPSTone technique to compare two texts—just as they used this technique to analyze individual texts in Chapter 3 and multiple texts in each of the last two examples. For this example, I have used two texts that say very different things about Martin Luther—a Catholic monk who lived in Germany during the 16th century. Beginning in 1517, Luther spoke out against a long list of church abuses, including the misuse of relics, the selling of indulgences, and the worldliness of the popes. Those who agreed with Luther and supported his Reformation praised his knowledge and wisdom, as this fellow Protestant did in 1518 (occasion):

> His sweetness in answering is remarkable, his patience in listening is incomparable . . . his answers, so brief, so wise, and drawn from the Holy Scriptures, easily made admirers of everyone who heard him. Our best men argued against him as hard as they could. However, they were unable to make him budge an inch from his propositions. He . . . is so devoted to the Bible and so suspicious of the antiquated theologians of our schools.
>
> Friar Martin Bucer
> Protestant reformer in Germany
> 1518
>
> *Source:* Smith, P. (Ed.) (1913). *Luther's Correspondence and Other Contemporary Letters: Vol. 1*. Philadelphia: The Luther Publication Society.

Obviously, Friar Bucer (speaker) was a great fan of Luther and his movement. Probably trying to convince other 16th-century reformers (audience) that Luther was a great spiritual leader (purpose), Bucer argued that Luther was extremely pious and knowledgeable (subject). Specifically, he said that Luther was "sweet," "remarkable," "wise," and "devoted to the Bible" (evidence). However, like Luther, Bucer was a German, a churchman, and a reformer. One wonders, was Bucer a friend of Luther's? Could his admiration have led him to exaggerate Luther's good qualities (and overlook his bad ones)? Was Luther really so sweet, so remarkable, so wise?

At least one person did not think so. Probably writing to convince other members of the Catholic clergy (audience) that Luther was a bad man (purpose), Sylvester Prierias (speaker), a 16th-century (occasion) Italian Catholic theologian, wrote:

> [Luther is] a leper and a loathsome fellow . . . a false libeler and calumniator . . . a dog and the son of a bitch, born to snap and bite at the sky with his canine mouth . . . with a brain of brass and a nose of iron.
>
> Sylvester Prierias
> Italian and Catholic theologian
> 16th century
>
> *Source:* Todd, J.M. (1982). *Luther: A Life*. New York: Crossroad Publishing Company.

Obviously, Prierias hated Luther. In this text, he argued that Luther was an abomination (subject), calling him a "leper," "a dog," "a false libeler," and a "son of a bitch" (evidence). But was Luther really a bad man, or did his teachings simply present a threat to the power and reputation of the Roman Catholic Church—and to Prierias himself? Prierias lived at the same time as Luther, but did Prierias really know him? The excerpt does not say; but, as Luther lived in Germany, it is conceivable that Prierias—an Italian—never saw him in the flesh or heard him speak. Also, since Luther wrote in German, it is possible that Prierias never even read his works.

So which of these two men was right? Was Luther a sweet, wise, and remarkable man, or was he a rotten S.O.B. whose false teachings led good Catholics astray? The truth is that Luther was probably not as bad as Prierias made him out to be or as saintly as Bucer described him. From our analysis of these two texts, it is safe to say that at least one person thought highly of Luther and at least one did not. However, if we wanted to acquire a more complete understanding of how people in 16th-century Europe reacted to Martin Luther and his teachings, we would need to analyze additional primary sources (additional members of the Catholic and Protestant clergy, people who were not connected with the clergy, and so on). We might want to consult the works of contemporary scholars who have broached this topic as well.

We can use a simple Venn Diagram (see Figure 4.3) to help students organize the information they are pulling out of each text and compare two texts successfully. While high school students may be able to organize all of their information (speaker, occasion, audience, purpose, subject, evidence, and tone) in a single diagram, elementary and middle school teachers may want students to complete seven separate diagrams in order to avoid confusion. Another graphic organizer we can use for this purpose is the one in Figure 4.4. This is simply a variation of a simple Venn Diagram. However, more so than a simple Venn Diagram, this graphic organizer allows students to easily and efficiently organize their information. For this reason, I prefer this graphic organizer to the diagram in Figure 4.3.

As our students begin comparing texts and working with multiple sources, it may help them to think of the texts they read as pieces of a puzzle. In a puzzle, every piece is important; but, by themselves, the pieces reveal very little about what the finished picture will look like. However, once all of the pieces have been put together, the whole picture becomes clear.

Historical documents are like this. By themselves, they can provide historians with useful but limited information about the event or topic they are researching. Collectively, however, their insight is much greater—even if a few of the "pieces" or interpretations are missing. Just as an old puzzle is likely to have a few of its pieces go missing with time, historians often have to draw their own conclusions about what happened with bits (or chunks) of information missing. For this reason, it is important for students to critically evaluate as many interpretations of the past as they can—including the interpretations of professional historians. A student conducting research for an essay on the life of Dr. Martin Luther King, Jr., for example, should consult as many biographies of King as he or she can find. Primary sources, such as letters written by King to others while he was in prison or public

Figure 4.3 Venn Diagram

Working With Multiple Texts

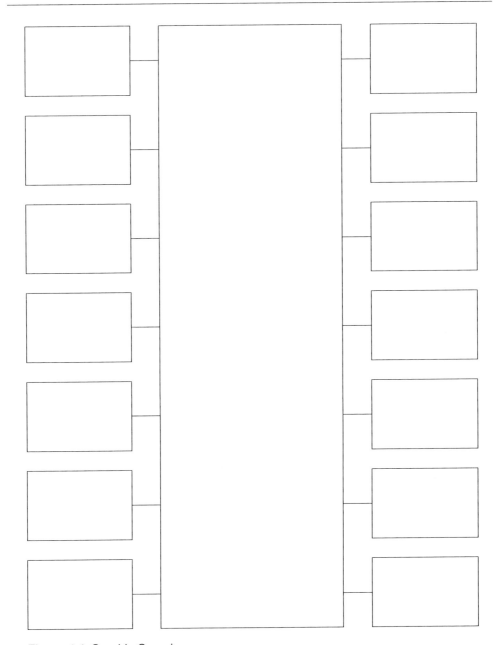

Figure 4.4 Graphic Organizer

speeches he gave (such as the famous "I Have A Dream" speech) are also a must, as are any writings by friends, family members, and opponents. Only after consulting sources written from so many different points of view does a student have enough "pieces" of King's world to really begin to understand his life.

Have Students Create Their Own Text-Based Questions

We can help students who are struggling to understand how sources written from different points of view work together to answer a question or solve a problem by having them create their own TBQ—either about something entirely outside the required curriculum or about something students are currently studying in class. This means that students will have to formulate a question about a topic of our choosing (or theirs, if we want them to pick a topic of personal interest to them) and then go out and find texts that directly relate to the question (just as they would if they were writing a research paper). When I use this strategy in my own classes, I usually select a topic for my students, as this allows me to create some specific guidelines they must follow and helps ensure that the TBQs they write are of good quality.

Take, for example, the following assignment, which I give my students during the first half of the school year. For this assignment, students are to create a TBQ about various stakeholders' reactions to our school during the current academic year. Before they begin working, however, I provide them with a list of rules, or guidelines, they must follow when creating their TBQ:

- You must interview at least six different people who are somehow connected to our school. This can include teachers, students, parents, administrators, alumni, community members, and other stakeholders.
- You must incorporate as many different points of view as possible. This means that you should interview as many different types of stakeholders (parents, teachers, students, etc.) as you can.
- You must have at least two texts that constitute negative reactions to our school, and at least two texts that constitute positive reactions. For this reason, you may have to interview more than six people to get the six texts required of you.
- After you have conducted all of your interviews, you must decide which six to include in your TBQ. As you are trying to decide, think about this: Which sources have backed up their reactions with specific evidence? Are there two or more sources that say similar things? Does one source support something said by another source? Do any sources directly contradict each other? Do all of the students you interviewed feel one way about our school, and all of the teachers/administrators another?
- You must format your TBQ so that it resembles the TBQs we have completed in class. In other words, you must identify and number your sources and write down exactly what they've told you. Do not simply summarize

or paraphrase what they said. Go back and look at some of the TBQs we've done in the past to help you format your TBQ correctly.

Obviously, the nature of this question requires that students conduct their interviews and create their TBQs outside of class. However, other create-your-own-TBQ assignments can easily be completed during class time, perhaps over two or three days. Of course, if students are creating a TBQ about content they are currently studying, they will need access to print or electronic sources to complete this activity successfully. In this case, we may want to create some guidelines about what types of sources they can use (visual and nonvisual, primary and secondary) and how many of these sources can come from print or electronic media. Once students have finished creating their own TBQs, we can have students trade TBQs with one another and, using the texts, answer each other's questions.

This assignment is great for helping all students, but especially struggling students, understand why we need multiple sources, each written from a different point of view, to completely (or more completely) answer a question or solve a problem. Additionally, by forcing students to conduct their own research and select the texts they will use to create their own text-based question, we improve their ability to compare texts to one another and understand how one text fills in gaps left by another. We also help them to recognize what perspective(s) or "pieces" of text are missing from the "puzzle" and how to seek out missing information in order to complete the "picture." Last, but not least, we help them to become proficient at evaluating different types of sources—determining to what degree those sources may be credible.

Integrating Information from Different Types of Sources

Eventually, of course, we want students to become adept at working with multiple visual and nonvisual texts (including primary and secondary sources) simultaneously. The strategies presented in this chapter will go a long way in helping students acquire the skills they need to integrate information from different types of nonfiction text. When we feel that our students are ready to tackle TBQs that are based on a variety of text types, we can briefly have them return to comparing two sources—visual and nonvisual or primary and secondary. For instance, a fourth or fifth grade teacher could have students compare a first-hand account of African-American ballplayers in the Negro Leagues to a second-hand account of their treatment found in *We Are the Ship: The Story of Negro League Baseball* (Nelson, 2008); a middle school teacher could have students construct a holistic picture of the history of Manhattan by comparing the information from Donald Mackay's *The Building of Manhattan* (1987) with one of the multimedia resources available in the "Manhattan on the Web" portal hosted by the New York Public Library. Then, we can go back to having students work with multiple sources, incorporating at least one primary and secondary source, and one visual and nonvisual source, into the TBQ. Over time, we can increase the number of different types of sources we require students to analyze.

The following TBQ incorporates a number of visual, nonvisual, primary, and secondary sources and is one I give students in my own classes during the second half of the school year:

Text-Based Questions

Using the following texts, analyze the causes, characteristics, and consequences of the Black Death outbreak that occurred in Europe between 1347 and 1351. Are there any additional texts that would help you to further assess the historical significance of the Black Death during this period?

Text #1

Source: Janu, B.D. (2000). *Bring Out Your Dead! Recreating the Black Death in the Classroom.* Bell, Book, and Camera Productions. *www.bellbookcamera.com*

Working With Multiple Texts

Text #2

In the year of our Lord 1348, there happened at Florence, the finest city in all Italy, a most terrible plague; which, whether owing to the influence of the planets, or that it was sent from God as a just punishment for our sins, had broken out some years before in [the east], and after passing from place to place, and making incredible havoc all the way, had now reached the west. There, in spite of all the means that art and human foresight could suggest, such as keeping the city clear from filth, the exclusion of all suspected persons, and the publication of copious instructions for the preservation of health; and notwithstanding manifold humble supplications offered to God in processions and otherwise; it began to show itself in the spring . . .

Here there appeared certain tumors in the groin or under the arm-pits, some as big as a small apple, others as an egg; and afterwards purple spots in most parts of the body; in some cases large but few in number, in others smaller and more numerous—both sorts the usual messengers of death. To the cure of this malady, neither medical knowledge nor the power of drugs was of any effect; whether because the disease was in its own nature mortal, or that the physicians . . . could form no just idea of the cause, nor consequently devise a true method of cure . . . Nearly all died the third day from the first appearance of the symptoms, some sooner, some later, without any fever or other accessory symptoms . . . It spread daily, like fire . . .

Source: Boccaccio, G. (1351 [1855]). *The Decameron* (trans. W.K. Kelly). London: Henry G. Bohn.

Text #3

In the year 1349 there occurred the greatest epidemic that ever happened. Death went from one end of the earth to the other . . . This epidemic also came to Strasbourg . . . and it is estimated that about sixteen thousand people died.

In the matter of this plague the Jews throughout the world were reviled and accused in all lands of having caused it through the poison which they are said to have put into the water and the wells—that is what they were accused of—and for this reason the Jews were burnt all the way from the Mediterranean into Germany . . .

Source: "The Cremation of the Strasbourg Jews" by Jacob von Konigshofen (1347–1420). In Marcus, J.R. (1938). *The Jew in the Medieval World: A Source Book, 315–1791*. New York: Union of American Hebrew Congregations.

Text #4

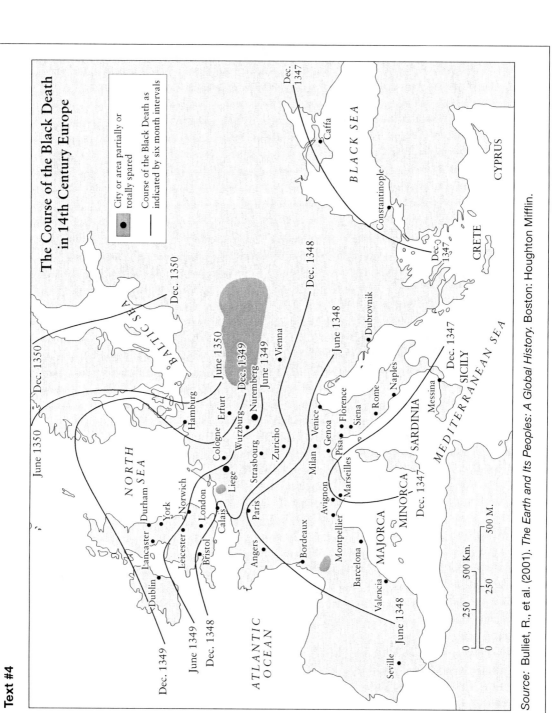

Source: Bulliet, R., et al. (2001). *The Earth and Its Peoples: A Global History*. Boston: Houghton Mifflin.

Text #5

Source: *The Triumph of Death* by Pieter Bruegel (1562). Image retrieved from *http://en.wikipedia.org/wiki/The_Triumph_of_Death*

Text #6

Region	Population Loss
Belgium/Luxembourg	1.2
England/Wales	1.2
France	4.8
Holy Roman Empire	4.5
Ireland	0.2
Italy	3.0
Scotland	0.1
Spain	2.0

Note: Total population in Europe before the outbreak = 53.2 million

Source: Table showing population loss (in millions) in Europe as a result of plague outbreaks between 1347 and 1351. Data retrieved from Dunnigan, J. & Nofi, A. (1994). *Medieval Life and the Hundred Years War.* DENO Partnership. *http://hyw.com/books/history/1_help_c.htm*

As you can see, this TBQ incorporates a number of different types of sources. There are several primary and secondary sources. Three of the texts are visuals, and three of the texts are nonvisuals. One of the visuals is a map, and one of the nonvisuals is a table. The texts differ in length and complexity, but they all directly relate to the question. The texts complement each other and are all important pieces of the puzzle. While we could certainly include many more texts in the TBQ, eliminating any one of them without finding a suitable replacement would make it very difficult for students to answer the question. Each of the texts identifies at least one cause, characteristic, or consequence of the Black Death; and there are at least two texts that directly address causes (1 and 2), two texts that directly address characteristics (2 and 4), and three texts that directly address consequences (3, 5, and 6). Plague was caused by a bacterium called *yersinia pestis*, which was carried by the rat flea (though some people during the Middle Ages believed it was caused by the movement of the planets or the Jews or was brought on by God as a punishment for sin); it spread along land and sea trade routes, was highly contagious, and caused a number of terrible symptoms (such as lumps under the arm and purple spots all over the body); and it killed off approximately one-third of Western Europe's entire population. So many died in such a short period of time that it led to widespread fear and social unrest. Mass hysteria led to rash accusations, and thousands of innocent Jews were tortured and killed.

Tips for Creating a Good Text-Based Question

Ultimately, we want our students to answer TBQs like this one—TBQs that consist of multiple texts and incorporate a number of different types of sources. Of course, creating a TBQ like this one requires a fair bit of time and research, especially at first. It took me about four hours to create this TBQ five years ago, even with all the free resources available to me online. I wish I could say that I could show you how to create a great TBQ in 15 minutes, but I have never figured out how to come close to that myself! However, as with anything else, it gets easier with practice; and I have created a checklist of sorts you can use to help speed up the process (see Figure 4.5). More importantly, though, this checklist will provide you with some specific guidelines for creating good TBQs today—something that, I have learned, is more challenging than it seems.

> **TBQ Checklist for Teachers**
>
> **Question:**
>
> 1. Pick a topic. (In my last example, the topic of my TBQ was the Black Death.)
> 2. Determine what you want students to know about the topic. (For my TBQ on the Black Death, I wanted students to analyze *causes*, *characteristics*, and *consequences*.)
> 3. Formulate a question. (My question asked students to analyze the causes, characteristics, and consequences of the Black Death outbreak that occurred in Europe between 1347 and 1351. I also asked them to identify an additional text that they thought might help them to further assess the historical significance of the Black Death during this period.)
>
> **Sources:**
>
> 4. Now, find at least one text that addresses each part of your question. (When I wrote my TBQ, I included at least one text that addressed causes, at least one that addressed characteristics, and at least one that addressed consequences of the Black Death outbreak that occurred in Europe between 1347 and 1351. In fact, I included three texts in my TBQ that addressed consequences, simply because there were several major consequences of the Black Death that I wanted to cover.)
> 5. Once you have found the texts that you think you want to use, ask yourself the following questions: Did I use nothing but word-based text? Did I incorporate various types of text (visual and nonvisual, primary and secondary)? Do the texts complement each other? Does one text fill in gaps left by another text? (For example, in my TBQ, texts 1 and 2 addressed different causes of the Black Death; texts 3, 5, and 6 addressed different consequences.) Remember that charts, graphs, tables, diagrams, and photographs are all great things to incorporate in your TBQ when appropriate.
> 6. Go back and revise your TBQ as necessary. Add sources, substitute one source for another—whatever you need to do.
>
> **Finishing Touches:**
>
> 7. Can students formulate a good, evidence-based response to your question by using the texts you have given them?
> 8. Did you identify your sources and number your texts?

Figure 4.5 TBQ Checklist For Teachers

Summary

Most of the work people do, both in college and on the job, requires them to analyze and evaluate multiple sources. Students in college have to analyze and evaluate a number of visual and nonvisual texts (including primary and secondary sources) in order to write their research papers. In the business world, employees have to analyze and evaluate data presented in a variety of different formats, including written reports, pie charts, bar graphs, spreadsheets, and databases in order to prepare their own reports, proposals, or presentations. Therefore, in order to be college- and career-ready in the 21st century, students need to learn how to synthesize information in addition to analyzing and evaluating individual texts. Specifically, they need to understand the relationship between texts and how they work together to answer a question or solve a problem. They need to be able to compare texts to one another and understand how one text fills in gaps left by another text. They need to know how to integrate background knowledge with knowledge they have gleaned from a text and recognize what perspective(s) or types of text are missing and would be helpful. Finally, students need to be able to formulate an argument, or thesis statement, in response to text-based questions and support their thesis with evidence from each one of the texts.

There are a number of strategies we can use to teach students how to analyze and evaluate multiple sources (and understand how they work together to answer a question). We can use the SOAPSTone technique, for example, to analyze texts connected to a fun and interesting topic outside the required curriculum—like school events, community athletics, favorite teachers, or national celebrities. We can use it to compare two texts—visual or nonvisual—and have students organize their information in a simple Venn Diagram (or, even better, a graphic organizer like the one in Figure 4.4). We can give students practice analyzing visual sources by having them group—or categorize—the texts and, working backwards, formulate their own question based on their "reading" of the visuals. We can also have students create their *own* TBQ—formulate a question, conduct their own research, and write a response. This activity is especially useful if students are struggling to understand how texts relate to one another or why we need multiple sources, written from different points of view, to completely (or more completely) answer a question or solve a problem.

These strategies—and others presented in this chapter—will go a long way in helping students acquire the analytical, synthesis, and evaluative skills they need to integrate information from different types of nonfiction texts; and once students master these skills, they will be able to handle just about any TBQ that we choose to throw at them. That is very empowering!

How might you use the strategies in this chapter to get your own students analyzing multiple texts (and integrate information from different types of sources)? Please feel free to write your ideas down here:

_____

_____

_____

References

Boccaccio, G. (1351 [1855]). *The Decameron* (trans. W.K. Kelly). London: Henry G. Bohn.

Bulliet, R., et al. (2001). *The Earth and Its Peoples: A Global History.* Boston: Houghton Mifflin.

Common Core State Standards Initiative (CCSSI). (2010, June). *Common Core State Standards for English Language Arts & Literacy in the History/Social Studies, Science, and Technical Subjects.* Retrieved from *www.corestandards.org/ELA-Literacy*

Dunnigan, J. & Nofi, A. (1994). *Medieval Life and the Hundred Years War.* DENO Partnership. Retrieved from *http://hyw.com/books/history/1_help_c.htm*

Janu, B.D. (2000). *Bring Out Your Dead! Recreating the Black Death in the Classroom.* Cary, IL: Bell, Book, and Camera Productions.

Mackay, D. (1987). *The Building of Manhattan.* New York: Harper and Row.

Marcus, J.R. (1938). *The Jew in the Medieval World: A Source Book, 315–1791.* New York: Union of American Hebrew Congregations.

Nelson, K. (2008). *We Are the Ship: The Story of Negro League Baseball.* New York: Jump at the Sun.

New York Public Library (n.d.). *Manhattan on the Web.* Retrieved from *http://legacy.www.nypl.org/branch/manhattan/index2.cfm?Trg=1&d1=865*

Smith, P. (Ed.) (1913). *Luther's Correspondence and Other Contemporary Letters: Vol. 1.* Philadelphia: The Luther Publication Society.

Todd, J.M. (1982). *Luther: A Life.* New York: Crossroad Publishing Company.

CHAPTER 5

Writing Good Responses to Text-Based Questions

Once students have learned how to use the SOAPSTone technique to analyze texts carefully (and understand how different types of sources can work together to answer a question or solve a problem), they must learn how to formulate good responses to text-based questions. Because thinking is clarified by writing, and because students must learn to communicate effectively, students need practice crafting sophisticated arguments and defending those arguments with text-based evidence.

The Common Core State Standards place a great deal of emphasis on writing about nonfiction texts (see Figure 5.1). In order to be college- and career-ready, the Standards say that students need to learn to "use writing as a way of offering and supporting opinions, demonstrating understanding of the subjects they are studying, and conveying real and imagined experiences and events." Students must learn to "appreciate that a key purpose of writing is to communicate clearly to an external, sometimes unfamiliar audience," and "adapt the form and content of their writing to accomplish a particular task and purpose." They must "develop the capacity to build knowledge on a subject through research projects and to respond analytically to literary and informational sources." To meet these goals, the Standards say that students must "devote significant time and effort to writing, producing numerous pieces over short and extended time frames throughout the year" (CCSSI, 2010).

Common Core Connection

ELA Writing Standards for Informational Text

Grade 3
W.3.2: Write informative/explanatory texts to examine a topic and convey ideas and information clearly.
W.3.2a: Introduce a topic and group related information together.

Figure 5.1 Common Core Grade Level Standards for Writing
Source: CCSSI, 2010

W.3.2b: Develop the topic with facts, definitions, and details.
W.3.2d: Provide a concluding statement or section.
W.3.4: With guidance and support from adults, produce writing in which the development and organization are appropriate to task and purpose.
W.3.7: Conduct short research projects that provide knowledge about a topic.
W.3.8: Gather information from print and digital sources; take brief notes on sources and sort evidence into provided categories.
W.3.10: Write routinely over extended time frames (time for reflection, research, and revision) and shorter time frames (a single sitting or a day or two) for a range of discipline-specific tasks, purposes, and audiences.

Grade 4
W.4.2: Write informative/explanatory texts to examine a topic and convey ideas and information clearly.
W.4.2a: Introduce a topic clearly and group related information in paragraphs and sections.
W.4.2b: Develop the topic with facts, definitions, and concrete details, quotations, and other information or examples related to the topic.
W.4.2e: Provide a concluding statement or section related to the information or explanation presented.
W.4.4: Produce clear and coherent writing in which the development and organization are appropriate to task, purpose, and audience.
W.4.5: With guidance and support from peers and adults, develop and strengthen writing as needed by planning, revising, and editing.
W.4.7: Conduct short research projects that build knowledge through investigation of different aspects of a topic.
W.4.8: Gather relevant information from print and digital sources; take notes and categorize information, and provide a list of sources.
W.4.9: Draw evidence from literary or informational texts to support analysis, reflection, and research.
W.4.10: Write routinely over extended time frames (time for research, reflection, and revision) and shorter time frames (a single day or two) for a range of discipline-specific tasks, purposes, and audiences.

Grade 5
W.5.2: Write informative/explanatory texts to examine a topic and convey ideas and information clearly.
W.5.2a: Introduce a topic clearly, provide a general observation and focus, and group related information logically.
W.5.2b: Develop the topic with facts, definitions, concrete details, quotations, or other information and examples related to the topic.
W.5.2e: Provide a concluding statement or section related to the information or explanation presented.
W.5.4: Produce clear and coherent writing in which the development and organization are appropriate to task, purpose, and audience.
W.5.5: With guidance and support from peers and adults, develop and strengthen writing as needed by planning, revising, editing, rewriting, or trying a new approach.
W.5.7: Conduct short research projects that use several sources to build knowledge through investigation of different aspects of a topic.
W.5.8: Gather relevant information from print and digital sources; summarize or paraphrase information in notes and finished work, and provide a list of sources.
W.5.9: Draw evidence from literary or informational texts to support analysis, reflection, and research.

Figure 5.1 (*Continued*)

W.5.10: Write routinely over extended time frames (time for research, reflection, and revision) and shorter time frames (a single day or two) for a range of discipline-specific tasks, purposes, and audiences.

Grade 6
W.6.1: Write arguments to support claims with clear reasons and relevant arguments.
W.6.1a: Introduce claim(s) and organize the reasons and evidence clearly.
W.6.1b: Support claim(s) with clear reasons and relevant evidence, using credible sources and demonstrating an understanding of the topic or text.
W.6.2: Write informative/explanatory texts to examine a topic and convey ideas, concepts, and information through the selection, organization, and analysis of relevant content.
W.6.2a: Introduce a topic; organize ideas, concepts, and information, using strategies such as definition, classification, comparison/contrast, and cause/effect.
W.6.2b: Develop the topic with relevant facts, definitions, concrete details, quotations, or other information and examples.
W.6.2e: Establish and maintain a formal style.
W.6.2f: Provide a concluding statement or section that follows from the information or explanation presented.
W.6.4: Produce clear and coherent writing in which the development, organization, and style are appropriate to task, purpose, and audience.
W.6.5: With some guidance and support from peers and adults, develop and strengthen writing as needed by planning, revising, editing, rewriting, or trying a new approach.
W.6.7: Conduct short research projects to answer a question, drawing on several sources and refocusing the inquiry when appropriate.
W.6.8: Gather relevant information from multiple print and digital sources; assess the credibility of each source; and quote or paraphrase the data and conclusions of others while avoiding plagiarism and providing basic bibliographic information from sources.
W.6.9: Draw evidence from literary or informational texts to support analysis, reflection, and research.
W.6.10: Write routinely over extended time frames (time for research, reflection, and revision) and shorter time frames (a single day or two) for a range of discipline-specific tasks, purposes, and audiences.

Grade 7
W.7.1: Write arguments to support claims with clear reasons and relevant evidence.
W.7.1a: Introduce claim(s), acknowledge alternate or opposing claims, and organize the reasons and evidence logically.
W.7.1b: Support claim(s) with logical reasoning and relevant evidence, using accurate, credible sources and demonstrating an understanding of the topic or text.
W.7.2: Write informative/explanatory texts to examine a topic and convey ideas, concepts, and information through the selection, organization, and analysis of relevant content.
W.7.2a: Introduce a topic clearly, previewing what is to follow; organize ideas, concepts, and information using strategies such as definition, classification, comparison/contrast, and cause/effect.
W.7.2b: Develop the topic with relevant facts, definitions, concrete details, quotations, or other information and examples.
W.7.2e: Establish and maintain a formal style.
W.7.2f: Provide a concluding statement or section that follows from and supports the explanation or information presented.
W.7.4: Produce clear and coherent writing in which the development, organization, and style are appropriate to task, purpose, and audience.
W.7.5: With some guidance and support from peers and adults, develop and strengthen writing as needed by planning, revising, editing, rewriting, or trying a new approach, focusing on how well purpose and audience have been addressed.

Figure 5.1 (*Continued*)

W.7.7: Conduct short research projects to answer a question, drawing on several sources and generating additional related, focused questions for further research and investigation.

W.7.8: Gather relevant information from multiple print and digital sources; assess the credibility and accuracy of each source; and quote or paraphrase the data and conclusions of others while avoiding plagiarism and following a standard format for citation.

W.7.9: Draw evidence from literary or informational texts to support analysis, reflection, and research.

W.7.10: Write routinely over extended time frames (time for research, reflection, and revision) and shorter time frames (a single day or two) from a range of discipline-specific tasks, purposes, and audiences.

Grade 8

W.8.1: Write arguments to support claims with clear reasons and relevant evidence.

W.8.1a: Introduce claim(s), acknowledge and distinguish the claim(s) from alternate or opposing claims, and organize the reasons and evidence logically.

W.8.1b: Support claim(s) with logical reasoning and relevant evidence, using accurate, credible sources and demonstrating an understanding of the topic or text.

W.8.2: Write informative/explanatory texts to examine a topic and convey ideas, concepts, and information through the selection, organization, and analysis of relevant content.

W.8.2a: Introduce a topic clearly, previewing what is to follow; organize ideas, concepts, and information into broader categories.

W.8.2b: Develop the topic with well-chosen facts, definitions, concrete details, quotations, or other information and examples.

W.8.2e: Establish and maintain a formal style.

W.8.2f: Provide a concluding statement or section that follows from and supports the information or explanation presented.

W.8.4: Produce clear and coherent writing in which the development, organization, and style are appropriate to task, purpose, and audience.

W.8.5: With some guidance and support from peers and adults, develop and strengthen writing as needed by planning, revising, editing, rewriting, or trying a new approach, focusing on how well purpose and audience have been addressed.

W.8.7: Conduct short research projects to answer a question (including a self-generated question), drawing on several sources and generating additional related, focused questions that allow for multiple avenues of exploration.

W.8.8: Gather relevant information from multiple print and digital sources; assess the credibility and accuracy of each source; and quote or paraphrase the data and conclusions of others while avoiding plagiarism and following a standard format for citation.

W.8.9: Draw evidence from literary or informational texts to support analysis, reflection, and research.

W.8.10: Write routinely over extended time frames (time for research, reflection, and revision) and shorter time frames (a single day or two) from a range of discipline-specific tasks, purposes, and audiences.

Grades 9–10

W.9–10.1: Write arguments to support claims in an analysis of substantive topics or texts, using valid reasoning and relevant and sufficient evidence.

W.9–10.1a: Introduce precise claim(s), distinguish the claim(s) from alternate or opposing claims, and create an organization that establishes clear relationships among claim(s), counterclaims, reasons, and evidence.

W.9–10.1b: Develop claim(s) and counterclaims fairly, supplying evidence for each while pointing out the strengths and limitations of both in a manner that anticipates the audience's knowledge level and concerns.

W.9–10.2: Write informative/explanatory texts to examine and convey complex ideas, concepts, and information clearly and accurately through the effective selection, organization, and analysis of content.

Figure 5.1 (*Continued*)

W.9–10.2a: Introduce a topic; organize complex ideas, concepts, and information to make important connections and distinctions.
W.9–10.2b: Develop the topic with well-chosen, relevant, and sufficient facts, definitions, concrete details, quotations, or other information and examples appropriate to the audience's knowledge of the topic.
W.9–10.2e: Establish and maintain a formal style and objective tone while attending to the norms and conventions of the discipline in which they are writing.
W.9–10.2f: Provide a concluding statement or section that follows from and supports the information or explanation presented.
W.9–10.4: Produce clear and coherent writing in which the development, organization, and style are appropriate to task, purpose, and audience.
W.9–10.5: Develop and strengthen writing as needed by planning, revising, editing, rewriting, or trying a new approach, focusing on addressing what is most significant for a specific purpose and audience.
W.9–10.7: Conduct short as well as more sustained research projects to answer a question (including a self-generated question) or solve a problem; narrow to broaden the inquiry when appropriate; synthesize multiple sources on the subject, demonstrating understanding of the subject under investigation.
W.9–10.8: Gather relevant information from multiple authoritative print and digital sources; assess the usefulness of each source in answering the research question; integrate information into the text selectively to maintain the flow of ideas, avoiding plagiarism and following a standard format for citation.
W.9–10.9: Draw evidence from literary or informational texts to support analysis, reflection, and research.
W.9–10.10: Write routinely over extended time frames (time for research, reflection, and revision) and shorter time frames (a single day or two) from a range of discipline-specific tasks, purposes, and audiences.

Grades 11–12
W.11–12.1: Write arguments to support claims in an analysis of substantive topics or texts, using valid reasoning and relevant and sufficient evidence.
W.11–12.1a: Introduce precise, knowledgeable claim(s), establish the significance of the claim(s), distinguish the claim(s) from alternate or opposing claims, and create an organization that logically sequences claim(s), counterclaims, reasons, and evidence.
W.11–12.1b: Develop claim(s) and counterclaims fairly and thoroughly, supplying the most relevant evidence for each while pointing out the strengths and limitations of both in a manner that anticipates the audience's knowledge level, concerns, values, and possible biases.
W.11–12.2: Write informative/explanatory texts to examine and convey complex ideas, concepts, and information clearly and accurately through the effective selection, organization, and analysis of content.
W.11–12.2a: Introduce a topic; organize complex ideas, concepts, and information so that each new element builds on that which precedes it to create a unified whole.
W.11–12.2b: Develop the topic thoroughly by selecting the most significant and relevant facts, extended definitions, concrete details, quotations, or other information and examples appropriate to the audience's knowledge of a topic.
W.11–12.2e: Establish and maintain a formal style and objective tone while attending to the norms and conventions of the discipline in which they are writing.
W.11–12.2f: Provide a concluding statement or section that follows from and supports the argument presented.
W.11–12.4: Produce clear and coherent writing in which the development, organization, and style are appropriate to task, purpose, and audience.
W.11–12.5: Develop and strengthen writing as needed by planning, revising, editing, rewriting, or trying a new approach, focusing on addressing what is most significant for a specific purpose and audience.

Figure 5.1 (*Continued*)

W.11–12.7: Conduct short as well as more sustained research projects to answer a question (including a self-generated question) or solve a problem; narrow or broaden the inquiry when appropriate; synthesize multiple sources on the subject, demonstrating understanding of the subject under investigation.

W.11–12.8: Gather relevant information from multiple authoritative print and digital sources; assess the strengths and limitations of each source in terms of the task, purpose, and audience; integrate information into the text selectively to maintain the flow of ideas, avoiding plagiarism and overreliance on any one source and following a standard format for citation.

W.11–12.9: Draw evidence from literary or informational texts to support analysis, reflection, and research.

W.11–12.10: Write routinely over extended time frames (time for research, reflection, and revision) and shorter time frames (a single day or two) from a range of discipline-specific tasks, purposes, and audiences.

History/Social Studies, Science, and Technical Writing Standards

Grades 6–8

WHST.6–8.1: Write arguments focused on discipline-specific content.

WHST.6–8.1a: Introduce claim(s) about a topic or issue, acknowledge and distinguish the claim(s) from alternative or opposing claims, and organize the reasons and evidence logically.

WHST.6–8.1b: Support claim(s) with logical reasoning and relevant, accurate data and evidence that demonstrates an understanding of the topic or text, using credible sources.

WHST.6–8.2: Write informative/explanatory texts, including the narration of historical events, scientific procedures/experiments, or technical processes.

WHST.6–8.2a: Introduce a topic clearly, previewing what is to follow; organize ideas, concepts, and information into broader categories as appropriate to achieving purpose.

WHST.6–8.2b: Develop the topic with relevant, well-chosen facts, definitions, concrete details, quotations, or other information and examples.

WHST.6–8.2e: Establish and maintain a formal style and objective tone.

WHST.6–8.2f: Provide a concluding statement or section that follows from and supports the information or explanation presented.

WHST.6–8.4: Produce clear and coherent writing in which the development, organization, and style are appropriate to task, purpose, and audience.

WHST.6–8.5: With some guidance and support from peers and adults, develop and strengthen writing as needed by planning, revising, editing, rewriting, or trying a new approach, focusing on how well purpose and audience have been addressed.

WHST.6–8.7: Conduct short research projects to answer a question (including a self-generated question), drawing on several sources and generating additional related, focused questions that allow for multiple avenues of exploration.

WHST.6–8.8: Gather relevant information from multiple print and digital sources; assess the credibility and accuracy of each source; and quote or paraphrase the data and conclusions of others while avoiding plagiarism and following a standard format for citation.

WHST.6–8.9: Draw evidence from informational texts to support analysis, reflection, and research.

WHST.6–8.10: Write routinely over extended time frames (time for research, reflection, and revision) and shorter time frames (a single day or two) from a range of discipline-specific tasks, purposes, and audiences.

Grades 9–10

WHST.9–10.1: Write arguments focused on discipline-specific content.

WHST.9–10.1a: Introduce precise claim(s), distinguish the claim(s) from alternate or opposing claims, and create an organization that establishes clear relationships among the claim(s), counterclaims, reasons, and evidence.

Figure 5.1 (*Continued*)

WHST.9–10.1b: Develop claim(s) and counterclaims fairly, supplying data and evidence for each while pointing out the strengths and limitations of both claim(s) and counterclaims in a discipline-appropriate form and in a manner that anticipates the audience's knowledge level and concerns.

WHST.9–10.2: Write informative/explanatory texts, including the narration of historical events, scientific procedures/experiments, or technical processes.

WHST.9–10.2a: Introduce a topic and organize ideas, concepts, and information to make important connections and distinctions.

WHST.9–10.2b: Develop the topic with well-chosen, relevant, and sufficient facts, extended definitions, concrete details, quotations, or other information and examples appropriate to the audience's knowledge of the topic.

WHST.9–10.2e: Establish and maintain a formal style and objective tone while attending to the norms and conventions of the discipline in which they are writing.

WHST.9–10.2f: Provide a concluding statement or section that follows from and supports the information or explanation presented (e.g., articulating implications or significance of the topic).

WHST.9–10.4: Produce clear and coherent writing in which the development, organization, and style are appropriate to task, purpose, and audience.

WHST.9–10.5: Develop and strengthen writing as needed by planning, revising, editing, rewriting, or trying a new approach, focusing on what is most significant for a specific purpose and audience.

WHST.9–10.7: Conduct short as well as more sustained research projects to answer a question (including a self-generated question) or solve a problem; narrow or broaden the inquiry when appropriate; synthesize information from multiple sources on the subject, demonstrating understanding of the subject under investigation.

WHST.9–10.8: Gather relevant information from multiple authoritative print and digital sources; assess the usefulness of each source in answering the research question; integrate information into the text selectively to maintain the flow of ideas, avoiding plagiarism and following a standard format for citation.

WHST.9–10.9: Draw evidence from informational texts to support analysis, reflection, and research.

WHST.9–10.10: Write routinely over extended time frames (time for research, reflection, and revision) and shorter time frames (a single day or two) from a range of discipline-specific tasks, purposes, and audiences.

Grades 11–12

WHST.11–12.1: Write arguments focused on discipline-specific content.

WHST.11–12.1a: Introduce precise claim(s), distinguish the claim(s) from alternate or opposing claims, and create an organization that establishes clear relationships among the claim(s), counterclaims, reasons, and evidence.

WHST.11–12.1b: Develop claim(s) and counterclaims fairly, supplying data and evidence for each while pointing out the strengths and limitations of both claim(s) and counterclaims in a discipline-appropriate form and in a manner that anticipates the audience's knowledge level, concerns, values, and possible biases.

WHST.11–12.2: Write informative/explanatory texts, including the narration of historical events, scientific procedures/experiments, or technical processes.

WHST.11–12.2a: Introduce a topic and organize complex ideas, concepts, and information so that each new element builds on that which precedes it to create a unified whole.

WHST.11–12.2b: Develop the topic thoroughly by selecting the most significant and relevant facts, extended definitions, concrete details, quotations, or other information and examples appropriate to the audience's knowledge of the topic.

WHST.11–12.2e: Provide a concluding statement or section that follows from and supports the information or explanation provided (e.g., articulating implications or the significance of a topic).

WHST.11–12.4: Produce clear and coherent writing in which the development, organization, and style are appropriate to task, purpose, and audience.

Figure 5.1 (*Continued*)

WHST.11–12.5: Develop and strengthen writing as needed by planning, revising, editing, rewriting, or trying a new approach, focusing on what is most significant for a specific purpose and audience.
WHST.11–12.7: Conduct short as well as more sustained research projects to answer a question (including a self-generated question) or solve a problem; narrow or broaden the inquiry when appropriate; synthesize information from multiple sources on the subject, demonstrating understanding of the subject under investigation.
WHST.11–12.8: Gather relevant information from multiple authoritative print and digital sources; assess the usefulness of each source in answering the research question; integrate information into the text selectively to maintain the flow of ideas, avoiding plagiarism and overreliance on any one source and following a standard format for citation.
WHST.11–12.9: Draw evidence from informational texts to support analysis, reflection, and research.
WHST.11–12.10: Write routinely over extended time frames (time for research, reflection, and revision) and shorter time frames (a single day or two) from a range of discipline-specific tasks, purposes, and audiences.

Figure 5.1 (*Continued*)

Multiple-Choice vs. Free-Response Questions

While multiple-choice questions are always easiest for teachers to grade, we must resist the temptation to overuse multiple-choice questions as a way of assessing students' ability to analyze and evaluate nonfiction texts. Of course, that does not mean that we *cannot* write TBQs as multiple-choice questions. At first, depending on the age of our students or the nature of the question, it may be appropriate or necessary to have students select a response from a list of possible answers. In fact, I often include a few multiple-choice questions on each of my assessments—TBQs that require students to analyze or evaluate one or more texts related to topics they have recently studied.

For example, students in my global history classes are required to answer this TBQ early in the year, which I wrote in the form of two multiple-choice questions:

All who denied being Christians I considered should be [set free], because they called upon the gods at my dictation and did reverence, with incense and wine, to your image which I had ordered to be brought forward for this purpose, together with the statues of the deities . . . They all worshipped your image and the statues of the gods and cursed Christ.
Pliny the Younger (62–113 AD)
Christians in Bithynia

Source: Bettenson, H. & Maunder, C. (Eds.). (1999). *Documents of the Early Christian Church* (3rd ed.). Oxford: Oxford University Press.

1. The passage above, written by Pliny the Younger around 112 AD, suggests that Christians were persecuted by the Roman Empire because they:
   a. Drank wine during religious rituals and enjoyed the smell of incense.
   b. Cursed Christ and worshipped statues of false gods.
   c. Refused to worship the Roman Emperor.
   d. Entered Bithynia.

2. A reading of this passage would lead one to conclude that Pliny the Younger was probably:
   a. Sympathetic to Christians being persecuted by the Roman Empire.
   b. A Roman official seeking the emperor's counsel about trying accused Christians.
   c. A Roman citizen who had heard of Christianity but was completely unfamiliar with its beliefs.
   d. An emperor of Rome at a time when Christians were being persecuted.

A few weeks later, they begin to answer multiple-choice questions that require them to compare two or more sources:

Text #1

The persecution of Jews began in November 1348, and the first outbreak in Germany was at Solden, where all the Jews were burnt on the strength of a rumor that they had poisoned wells and rivers, as was afterwards confirmed by their own confessions and also by the confessions of Christians whom they had corrupted . . . Within the revolution of one year, that is from All Saints [1 November] 1348 until Michaelmas [29 September] 1349 all the Jews between Cologne and Austria were burnt and killed for this crime, young men and maidens and the old along with the rest. And blessed be God who confounded the ungodly who were plotting the extinction of his church.
  Heinrich Truchess, a former papal chaplain and canon of Constance.

Source: Lualdi, K.J. (Ed.) (2005). *Sources of the West: Peoples and Cultures*: Vol. 1 (2nd ed.). Boston: Bedford/St. Martin's Press.

Text #2

Very dear friends, all sorts of rumors are now flying about against Judaism and the Jews prompted by this unexpected and unparalleled mortality of Christians, which, alas, has raged in various parts of the world and is still woefully active in several places. Throughout our city, as in yours, many-winged Fame clamours that this mortality was initially caused, and is still being spread, by the poisonings of springs and wells, and that the Jews must have dropped poisonous substances in them. When it came to our knowledge that serious charges had been made against the Jews in several small towns and villages on the basis of this mortality, we sent numerous letters to you and to other cities and towns to uncover the truth behind these rumors, and set a thorough investigation in train . . . If a massacre of the Jews were allowed in the major cities (something which we are determined to prevent in our city, if we can, as long as the Jews are found to be innocent of these or similar actions) it could lead to the sort of outrages and disturbances which would whip up a popular revolt among the common people—and such revolts have in the past brought cities to misery and desolation. In any case, we are still of the opinion that this mortality and its attendant circumstances are caused by divine vengeance and nothing else. Accordingly we intend to forbid any harassment of the Jews in our city because of these flying rumors, but to defend them faithfully and keep them safe, as our predecessors did—and we are convinced that you ought to do the same.

From the Councillors of Cologne to Conrad von Winterthur to the Burgermeister and Councillors of Strassburg on 12 January 1349.

Source: Lualdi, K.J. (Ed.). (2005). *Sources of the West: Peoples and Cultures*: Vol. 1 (2nd ed.). Boston: Bedford/St. Martin's Press.

1. The second passage does not support the first passage because the second passage:
   a. Shows that Jews vastly outnumbered Christians in Western Europe.
   b. Falsely accuses Jews of starting the plague.
   c. Minimizes the devastating effects of the plague epidemic on Europe.
   d. Seeks to protect Jews from false accusation and persecution.

2. According to the passages, the Jews are being persecuted for all of the following reasons EXCEPT:
   a. They poisoned wells and rivers.
   b. They were believed to be responsible for starting the Black Death.
   c. Popular revolts had broken out in major German cities.
   d. Some Jews had confessed to committing crimes against Christians.

However, at the same time that my students are answering multiple-choice questions in class, they are also learning to answer TBQs that have been written as free-response questions. Of course, just as learning to analyze and evaluate texts is a process, learning to write analytically is a process. Just because students have already learned to write (or have even been told by their parents or other teachers that they are great writers) does not mean that they know how to write *analytically*. When students come into my global history classes as sophomores in high school, many of them believe (because they have performed well on FCAT Writes, our state's writing assessment) that they are phenomenal writers. In reality, nothing could be further from the truth. While my students may be good at writing for the FCAT, FCAT writing is neither formal nor analytical. Typically, prompts on the FCAT have been things like "Convince business leaders whether students should have a part-time job sometime during high school" or "Convince the principal whether or not eighth-grade students should be graded on how they behave in school." Obviously, these persuasive prompts are not text-based, do not require analytical thought, and do not require evidence-based responses. While I am not saying that these prompts are necessarily *bad*, they do not facilitate the kind of analytical writing that is required by Common Core and will get students ready for college and their careers.

Unfortunately, however, this is the kind of writing that students have become accustomed to in my state and in other states throughout the nation. Fortunately, the Common Core State Standards promise to change this by requiring students to write analytical essays in which they defend an argument with strong textual evidence. Students must learn to write formally, as objectively as possible, and gather information from multiple sources. They must learn to organize their essays in a way that is appropriate for nonfiction writing, and they must learn to cite their sources when they use them as evidence to support a claim. While this may seem like something that many of us would only have asked our high school students to do in the past (or, at the very least, students at the secondary level), Common Core expects all of us, including elementary teachers, to begin teaching our students these skills.

For example, a third-grader wrote the following response to a text-based question about why so many colonists died in Jamestown, an English colony established in Virginia in 1607 (see Figure 5.2). (Because this sample is for illustrative purposes, I have posted only an excerpt.)

When I first read this response, I was impressed that it had been written by a third-grade student. This TBQ consisted of multiple texts and included several different types of sources: an excerpt from two scholarly books; a graph showing the amount of rainfall in Jamestown between 1560 and 1650; a chart showing the occupations of the first Jamestown settlers; and a chronology of English mortality in Virginia between 1607 and 1610. These texts were certainly not written for a third-grade audience. In fact, I know a few teachers at my school who use this same TBQ with their *11th-grade* students; and, without the strategies I have presented in this book, they are hard pressed to get their students to

> 3rd Grade
>
> 1st 9 Weeks
>
> Why did so many colonists die in Jamestown? Dangers lie in the island of Jamestown. English colonist arrived in Jamestown a little island in the James river in Virginia in the year 1607. So why did so many colonists die?
> The reasons so many colonists died were environmental conditions, problems with Native Americans, lack of skills.
> The environmental conditions are that the water was brackish there was drought and disease. The reasons the water was that salt water mixed with the fresh water causing it to be undrinkable. Because of the drought the could not grow crops. The reason for the disease was that they didn't have toilets so they dumped their

Figure 5.2

write a response this good. Of course, this response is certainly far from perfect (even a third-grader can be taught to write a better response than this), and it is lacking in-text citations. Still, the fact that a third-grader understands the basic meaning of each of these texts, is using them collectively to answer a question, and is defending that answer with even a little evidence from each one of the texts (and under time constraints, no less!), shows us that *all* students (not just high school students) are capable of working toward mastery of these skills. If this student continues his or her work with TBQs, imagine how great a writer he or she will be by the time he or she graduates from high school.

Formulating a Thesis Statement

Of course, we, as teachers, know that a good essay consists of three major parts: an introduction, where the writer presents the argument he or she will make in the rest of the essay; a body, where the writer defends his or her argument with strong textual evidence; and a conclusion, where the writer briefly summarizes his or her argument and ties everything together. While many students also know that a good essay consists of these three parts, few are able to write a well-developed and well-organized essay without a lot of guidance and support from adults.

For this reason, it is important for us to guide students through the essay-writing process one step at a time. The first step in teaching students to write a good, analytical essay is to show them how to write a thesis statement. A thesis statement is a direct response to the question, the argument the writer will be defending in the body of the essay. The thesis statement usually appears near the end of the introductory paragraph and may consist of more than one sentence.

Writing Good Responses

In the previous example (see Figure 5.2), the thesis statement was very simple and consisted of a single sentence: "The reason so many colonists died were environmental conditions, problems with Native Americans, and lack of skills." It is a direct answer to the question "Why did so many colonists die in Jamestown?" It does not elaborate on *how* environmental conditions contributed to the death of colonists, or *what* skills the colonists were lacking that helped to contribute to their demise. This kind of information is reserved for the body of the student's essay because it is evidence he or she will use in support of his or her thesis.

To keep things simple, I am going to use one of the TBQs I presented in Chapter 4 for all of the examples that follow in this chapter:

Using the following texts, analyze the causes, characteristics, and consequences of the Black Death outbreak that occurred in Europe between 1347 and 1351. Are there any additional texts that would help you to further assess the historical significance of the Black Death during this period?

Source: Janu, B.D. (2000). *Bring Out Your Dead! Recreating the Black Death in the Classroom*. Bell, Book, and Camera Productions www.bellbookcamera.com

Text #2

In the year of our Lord 1348, there happened at Florence, the finest city in all Italy, a most terrible plague; which, whether owing to the influence of the planets, or that it was sent from God as a just punishment for our sins, had broken out some years before in [the east], and after passing from place to place, and making incredible havoc all the way, had now reached the west. There, in spite of all the means that art and human foresight could suggest, such as keeping the city clear from filth, the exclusion of all suspected persons, and the publication of copious instructions for the preservation of health; and notwithstanding manifold humble supplications offered to God in processions and otherwise; it began to show itself in the spring . . .

Here there appeared certain tumors in the groin or under the arm-pits, some as big as a small apple, others as an egg; and afterwards purple spots in most parts of the body; in some cases large but few in number, in others smaller and more numerous—both sorts the usual messengers of death. To the cure of this malady, neither medical knowledge nor the power of drugs was of any effect; whether because the disease was in its own nature mortal, or that the physicians . . . could form no just idea of the cause, nor consequently devise a true method of cure . . . Nearly all died the third day from the first appearance of the symptoms, some sooner, some later, without any fever or other accessory symptoms . . . It spread daily, like fire . . .

Source: Boccaccio, G. (1351 [1855]). *The Decameron* (trans. W.K. Kelly). London: Henry G. Bohn.

Text #3

In the year 1349 there occurred the greatest epidemic that ever happened. Death went from one end of the earth to the other . . . This epidemic also came to Strasbourg . . . and it is estimated that about sixteen thousand people died.

In the matter of this plague the Jews throughout the world were reviled and accused in all lands of having caused it through the poison which they are said to have put into the water and the wells—that is what they were accused of—and for this reason the Jews were burnt all the way from the Mediterranean into Germany . . .

Source: "The Cremation of the Strasbourg Jews" by Jacob von Konigshofen (1347–1420). In Marcus, J.R. (1938). *The Jew in the Medieval World: A Source Book, 315–1791*. New York: Union of American Hebrew Congregations.

Text #4

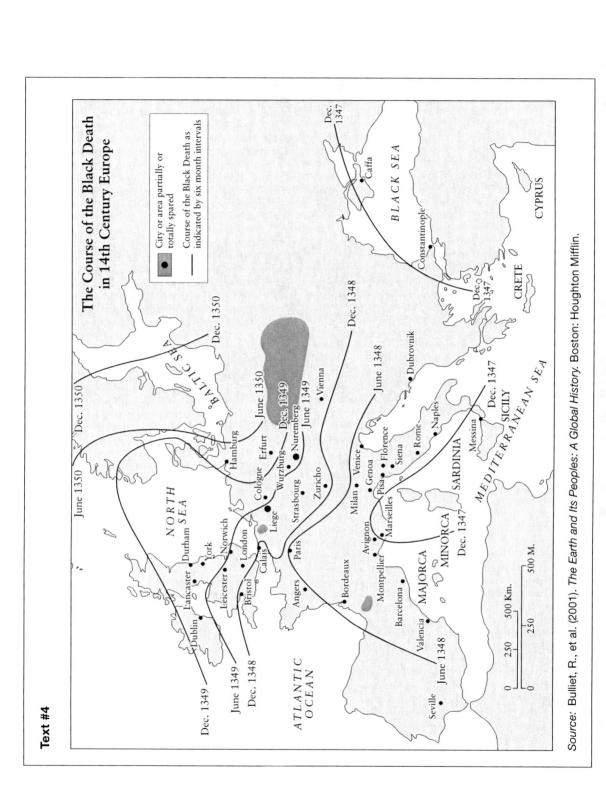

Source: Bulliet, R., et al. (2001). *The Earth and Its Peoples: A Global History*. Boston: Houghton Mifflin.

Text #5

Source: The Triumph of Death by Pieter Bruegel (1562). Image retrieved from *http://en.wikipedia.org/wiki/The_Triumph_of_Death*

Text #6

Region	Population Loss
Belgium/Luxembourg	1.2
England/Wales	1.2
France	4.8
Holy Roman Empire	4.5
Ireland	0.2
Italy	3.0
Scotland	0.1
Spain	2.0

Source: Table showing population loss (in millions) in Europe as a result of plague outbreaks between 1347 and 1351. Data retrieved from Dunnigan, J. & Nofi, A. (1994). *Medieval Life and the Hundred Years War*. DENO Partnership. *http://hyw.com/books/history/1_help_c.htm*

Note: Total population in Europe before the outbreak = 53.2 million

Once students have analyzed these texts using the SOAPSTone technique (and completed the handout depicted in Figure 5.3), we can have them practice writing a thesis statement that completely answers the question. In this case, students want to identify major causes, characteristics, and consequences of the Black Death outbreak that occurred in Europe between 1347 and 1351. The easiest way for students to do this is to make each one of their groupings a clause in their thesis. For instance, students may have grouped texts 1 and 2 together because they discussed several different causes of the Black Death: *yersinia pestis*, a bacterium spread by rat fleas (the real one), and the idea that the plague was caused by the movement of the planets, or was brought on by God as a punishment for sin (supposed causes). Students may have grouped texts 2 and 4 together because they both addressed characteristics of the Black Death (it spread along trade routes, was highly contagious, and caused a number of terrible symptoms) and texts 3, 5, and 6 together because they all addressed consequences (population loss, social unrest, and the murder of Jews). That being the case, students should write an introductory paragraph—with thesis statement—that looks something like this:

> Between 1347 and 1351, the Black Death ravaged Europe. Caused by a bacterium called yersinia pestis, which was carried by rat fleas (though some thought it was caused by the movement of the planets or was sent by God as a punishment for sin), the disease spread quickly along trade routes to virtually every part of the continent. So many people died in such a short period of time that it led to widespread fear and social unrest. Mass hysteria led to rash accusations, and thousands of innocent Jews were tortured and killed.

Notice that this thesis statement consists of two consecutive sentences (the second and third sentences of the introduction). It directly answers the question by identifying at least one specific cause, characteristic, and consequence of the Black Death, but it does not elaborate on *how* the rat flea transmitted the plague or *how* the plague spread along trade routes. It does not provide statistics on how many people died from the plague in different areas of Europe or describe the brutal treatment Christians inflicted on the Jews. It does, however, provide the reader with a road map for the rest of the essay and lays out the argument that the writer will be defending.

Writing Good Responses

The thesis statement should always appear in the introductory paragraph of a student's essay. In fact, the thesis may comprise the entirety of the introduction. While this paragraph begins with a short introductory statement (in order to identify the topic), it is not necessary for students to begin their essays with things like "Have you ever wondered what the causes and consequences of the Black Death were?" or to conclude their introduction with statements like "In this essay, I will tell you about the causes and consequences of the Black Death outbreak in Europe." In fact, these statements do not help to answer the question, detract from the overall quality of the essay, and should be avoided. Instead, students should write clearly and concisely (and without using passive voice), including only as many sentences as they need to in order to answer the question accurately and thoroughly.

With that said, the following examples are *not* good thesis statements:

> There were many causes, characteristics, and consequences of the Black Death. The Black Death was a horrible time in human history.

(Does not identify specific causes, characteristics, and consequences of the Black Death.)

> The Black Death broke out in Europe around 1347 and killed off about one-third of Western Europe's entire population. It had many causes, and some characteristics which I will be discussing in this essay.

(Identifies a consequence of the Black Death but does not identify a specific cause or characteristic. Furthermore, it uses the word "I," which is generally not appropriate in academic writing.)

> The Black Death, which broke out in Europe between 1347 and 1351, had some real and imagined causes. It caused a lot of death and destruction which has affected human society down to today.

(Is not specific enough and ends with a statement that is, at best, irrelevant.)

At first, it may be best to practice writing thesis statements as a class. However, as students become more comfortable formulating thesis statements, they can begin to do so on their own. To help students craft a good thesis statement, we can use a handout like the one in Figure 5.3. This handout is almost identical to the one in Figure 4.2, except that it includes space for students to write a thesis. My students find it helpful to have this completed handout in front of them when they sit down to write their thesis statements.

**TBQ—Multiple Text Analysis Worksheet:
SOAPSTone Technique**

1. Underline or circle important words or phrases in the question.

2. Are there any words or phrases in the question that you need to have defined for you? If so, write them here:
   _____
   _____
   _____

3. What do you already know about this topic?
   _____
   _____
   _____

4. Analyze each of one of the texts carefully using the SOAPSTone technique.

TEXT #1:

Speaker:_____
Occasion:_____
Audience:_____
Purpose:_____
Subject:_____
     Evidence #1: _____
     Evidence #2: _____
Tone: _____
Is it believable? Y/N Why or why not? _____

TEXT #2:

Speaker: _____
Occasion: _____
Audience: _____
Purpose: _____

Figure 5.3 Multiple Text Analysis Worksheet: SOAPSTone Technique

Subject: _____
        Evidence #1: _____
        Evidence #2: _____
Tone: _____
Is it believable? Y/N Why or why not? _____

TEXT #3:

Speaker: _____
Occasion: _____
Audience: _____
Purpose: _____
Subject: _____
        Evidence #1: _____
        Evidence #2: _____
Tone: _____
Is it believable? Y/N Why or why not? _____

TEXT #4:

Speaker: _____
Occasion: _____
Audience: _____
Purpose: _____
Subject: _____
        Evidence #1: _____
        Evidence #2: _____
Tone: _____
Is it believable? Y/N Why or why not? _____

TEXT #5:

Speaker: _____
Occasion: _____
Audience: _____
Purpose: _____
Subject: _____
        Evidence #1: _____
        Evidence #2: _____
Tone: _____
Is it believable? Y/N Why or why not? _____

TEXT #6:

Speaker: _____
Occasion: _____
Audience: _____
Purpose: _____

Figure 5.3 (*Continued*)

Subject: _____
        Evidence #1: _____
        Evidence #2: _____
Tone: _____
Is it believable? Y/N Why or why not? _____

TEXT #7:

Speaker: _____
Occasion: _____
Audience: _____
Purpose: _____
Subject: _____
        Evidence #1: _____
        Evidence #2: _____
Tone: _____
Is it believable? Y/N Why or why not? _____

TEXT #8:

Speaker: _____
Occasion: _____
Audience: _____
Purpose: _____
Subject: _____
        Evidence #1: _____
        Evidence #2: _____
Tone: _____
Is it believable? Y/N Why or why not? _____

TEXT #9:

Speaker: _____
Occasion: _____
Audience: _____
Purpose: _____
Subject: _____
        Evidence #1: _____
        Evidence #2: _____
Tone: _____
Is it believable? Y/N Why or why not? _____

5. Now, group the texts in as many appropriate ways as possible.

Texts _____ because _____
Texts _____ because _____
Texts _____ because _____
Texts _____ because _____

Figure 5.3 (*Continued*)

Writing Good Responses

> 6. What other text(s) would you find helpful for answering this question? Write your response here:
> _____
> _____
>
> 7. Finally, using the information you have gathered from the texts, write a thesis statement that answers the question:
> _____
> _____
> _____
> _____
> _____
> _____

Figure 5.3 (*Continued*)

Supporting the Thesis with Evidence

Once students have formulated their thesis statement, they must defend their thesis with evidence from each one of the texts. Since causes always precede consequences, it makes sense to make the second paragraph of the essay about causes. The third paragraph will be about characteristics, and the fourth paragraph will be about consequences. It is easy for students to organize their essay this way because they have already grouped the texts. Students will use evidence from texts 1 and 2 to address causes, evidence from texts 2 and 4 to address characteristics, and evidence from texts 3, 5, and 6 to address consequences. Since students have already identified the major causes of the Black Death in their thesis, all they have to do now is use specific words and phrases from texts 1 and 2 to elaborate on those causes. For example, a student might write a paragraph about causes that looks something like this:

> The Black Death was carried by fleas and rats. While some people believed the disease was <u>sent by God as a punishment for sin</u> (2), it was actually caused by fleas. <u>Yersinia pestis, the bacteria that causes plague, lives in the digestive tract of fleas. The flea infects the rat; and, when the rat dies, the flea has to find a new host</u> (1). Since humans and rats lived in close quarters during the Middle Ages, the fleas found humans to be a convenient alternative.

Notice that I have underlined information that comes directly from texts 1 and 2. In fact, this information is taken word-for-word from the texts; the texts are not summarized or paraphrased. To help students get used to supporting their claims with evidence, we may want to encourage them to take information word-for-word from the text (and even underline the evidence they use to support their thesis, as I have done). However, as students become more proficient at using individual texts to support their thesis, we should discourage them from over-quoting (and underlining their evidence) and encourage them, instead, to put evidence into their own words. For example, a student could write the same paragraph this way instead:

> The Black Death was carried by fleas and rats. While some people suspected that the plague was sent by God as a punishment for mankind's wicked deeds (2), it was actually caused by fleas. Fleas carried the bacterium yersinia pestis in their guts, and they infected the rat population of Western Europe. As the rat population died off from the plague, the fleas sought new hosts (1). Since humans and rats lived in close quarters during the Middle Ages, the fleas found humans to be a convenient alternative.

As you can see, this paragraph does not include direct quotes from texts 1 and 2. Instead, the writer pulls evidence from the texts to support his or her thesis but writes the paragraph using mostly his or her own words. The same is true for the paragraphs on characteristics and consequences:

> Once infected, plague victims developed a number of terrible symptoms: swellings in the groin or under the armpit and black and purple spots on the arms or thighs (2). The disease was highly contagious; and Boccaccio, an Italian writer, says that even the slightest contact with a diseased person could result in infection. Of course, the plague may have been worse in Florence, the town Boccaccio is describing, than in other places, and Boccaccio may have exaggerated the calamity in order to sell copies of his book. Nevertheless, the plague spread rapidly along maritime and overland trade routes until virtually the whole continent was infected. The plague had spread to Florence, Venice, Paris, and Marseilles by 1348; Strasbourg and London by 1349; and Erfurt by 1350 (4).
>
> Consequences of the Black Death included population loss, social chaos, and the murder of Jews. By the time the plague subsided in 1351, roughly one-third of Western Europe's population had been

wiped out. Individual populations decreased by millions over a few years. For example, 3 million people were killed in Italy, 4.8 million were killed in France, and 4.5 million were killed in the Holy Roman Empire (6). The confusion and fear that resulted from so much death led to rash accusations. In some places, Jews were blamed for the Black Death. Throughout Germany, thousands of Jews were burned alive by angry Christians who believed they had poisoned the water (3). Pieter Bruegel depicted the death, destruction, and general chaos that engulfed Western Europe in his painting "Triumph of Death" by showing streets filled with corpses and skeletons more numerous than the living (5). According to Bruegel's masterpiece, the plague struck men and women, rich and poor, adults and children, and members of the clergy. No one was safe. Of course, Bruegel made this painting in 1562, centuries after the epidemic in 1347 had subsided, so his depiction may be more based on legend than on actual fact (or, perhaps, depicts an outbreak of plague that occurred later, during the 16th century).

Citing Sources

In each of the last three paragraphs, the writer has used parenthetical citations to indicate which parts of his or her essay reference particular sources. We should always require our students to cite their sources in the body of their essays. Aside from helping students keep track of which sources they have used, it helps the reader identify which facts and ideas came from which sources. Furthermore, using simple parenthetical citations in response to text-based questions prepares students for the kind of citations they will have to make when writing research papers. Both the American Psychological Association (APA) and the Modern Language Association (MLA) require the use of in-text citations in scholarly papers. APA uses the author–date system, or the last name of the author and the year published, to help identify sources in the reference list. MLA uses the author-page method, which means that the author's last name and the page number(s) from which the quotation or paraphrase is taken appears in the text. If we want students to practice using one of these two formats, we can require them to cite their sources in the body of their essay, according to the rules of the MLA or APA manuals of style. On the other hand, if we simply want students to become accustomed to acknowledging their sources (beyond listing them in a bibliography at the end of their essay), we can have students write a text number, in parentheses, whenever they reference a particular source.

With that said, we should teach our students to place their citations only where there is a pause in the sentence—at the end of the sentence, before the period, or in the middle of the sentence, before a comma. If students are using evidence from one source in two or more consecutive sentences, then they need only cite the source one time—at the end of the first sentence in which they used it. On the other hand, as soon as another source is cited in the essay, students must re-cite the first source if they use it again.

Fortunately, teaching students to use in-text citations is easy. The rules are simple (especially if students are just citing a text number), and students usually get the hang of it with a little practice. At worst, we may have to remind students to place their citations whenever there is a pause in the sentence and discourage them from trying to cite multiple sources at once. For example, my students sometimes forget that they can place citations in the middle of sentences. For this reason, they sometimes put two text numbers in one set of parentheses (2, 4) at the end of a sentence, rather than citing one text in the middle of the sentence (2) and another at the end (4). We need to remind students to put only one text number in any given set of parentheses and cite their sources according to the rules we have laid out for them.

Incorporating Point of View

In their essays, students should demonstrate that they understand the biases of the authors and how the authors' respective backgrounds influence what they say. While incorporating an analysis of point of view in their essays is really not that difficult, students (at least my own students, and the students of other teachers I know) seem to make it hard. Over the years, I have found that the best way to help students learn to incorporate point of view in their essays is to insert their analysis right after they have finished using a particular text as evidence. If we want, we can require students to incorporate an analysis of point of view for every text they cite in order to help them become proficient at evaluating sources in their essays. However, we may want to require that students address point of view for two or three sources, depending on the age of our students and the nature of the question.

For example, in the last two paragraphs of our sample essay on the Black Death, the writer analyzes point of view twice, once after citing text #2 in paragraph three, and once after citing text #5 in paragraph four (I have underlined the point of view analysis in each of these two paragraphs):

> Once infected, plague victims developed a number of terrible symptoms: swellings in the groin or under the armpit and black and purple spots on the arms or thighs (2). The disease was highly contagious; and Boccaccio, an Italian writer, says that even the slightest contact with a diseased person could result in infection. Of course, <u>the plague may have been worse in Florence, the town</u>

> Boccaccio is describing, than in other places, and Boccaccio may have exaggerated the calamity in order to sell copies of his book. Nevertheless, the plague spread rapidly along maritime and overland trade routes until virtually the whole continent was infected. The plague had spread to Florence, Venice, Paris, and Marseilles by 1348; Strasbourg and London by 1349; and Erfurt by 1350 (4).
>
> Consequences of the Black Death included population loss, social chaos, and the murder of Jews. By the time the plague subsided in 1351, roughly one-third of Western Europe's population had been wiped out. Individual populations decreased by millions over a few years. For example, 3 million people were killed in Italy, 4.8 million were killed in France, and 4.5 million were killed in the Holy Roman Empire (6). The confusion and fear that resulted from so much death led to rash accusations. In some places, Jews were blamed for the Black Death. Throughout Germany, thousands of Jews were burned alive by angry Christians who believed they had poisoned the water (3). Pieter Bruegel depicted the death, destruction, and general chaos that engulfed Western Europe in his painting "Triumph of Death" by showing streets filled with corpses and skeletons more numerous than the living (5). According to Bruegel's masterpiece, the plague struck men and women, rich and poor, adults and children, and members of the clergy. No one was safe. Of course, Bruegel made this painting in 1562, centuries after the epidemic in 1347 had subsided, so his depiction may be more based on legend than on actual fact (or, perhaps, depicts an outbreak of plague that occurred later, during the 16th century).

Just as we teach students to underline their evidence when they first begin writing essays, we can teach students to underline or draw a circle around their analysis of point of view. Over time, of course, we want students to move away from labeling the different parts of their essays and become proficient at writing essays entirely on their own.

Writing a Conclusion

Last, but not least, students should briefly conclude their essay in a final paragraph. In many cases, a satisfactory conclusion need only restate what students wrote in their thesis. However, since my prompt on the Black Death requires students to suggest an additional text that could help them more completely answer the question, students writing this essay need to suggest an additional text as well. Of course, they could make this suggestion in the body of the essay; but I always teach my students to do so when they write their conclusion:

> Between 1347 and 1351, the Black Death (a terrible disease caused by yersinia pestis and carried by fleas and rats) spread quickly along trade routes to virtually every part of the continent. By 1351, one-third of Western Europe's entire population had been wiped out by the plague and thousands of Jews had been murdered. Useful additional texts could include testimonies from those who were infected, texts detailing economic consequences of the plague, and its impact on other works of art during this time period.

Like learning to cite sources, learning to write a conclusion is easy. My own students have very little trouble writing them, even as novices.

Additional Tips

As you begin the writing process with your students, remember that it takes time. Most students do not become adept at writing essays overnight, especially essays that require students to think analytically and support their arguments with text-based evidence. Also, expect that essays will (at least at first) be riddled with spelling or grammatical errors, fail to transition smoothly from one paragraph to the next, and be more superficial than the analysis students have conducted in class. That's okay. The purpose of this exercise is to acclimate students to writing formal, analytical essays. Students will become pros at writing essays with considerable time and practice.

The first few times your students practice essay-writing, I strongly recommend that you write their essays with them. As a class, you can write an essay together—the students, of course, providing input as you write out sentences on the board. Of course, each student should be writing down the essay the class generates on his or her own sheet of notebook paper in order to use the finished product as a guide for writing future TBQs by themselves.

You can also provide students with an essay that is partially complete and have them fill in the missing information on their own. For example, it could look like this:

Between 1347 and 1351, the Black Death ravaged Europe. Caused by _____

_____

_____, the disease spread quickly along trade routes to

Writing Good Responses

virtually every part of the continent. So many people died in such a short period of time that _____ _____.

The Black Death was carried by fleas and rats. While some people suspected that the plague _____ _____ (2), it was actually caused by fleas. _____ _____ _____ (1).

Once infected, plague victims developed a number of terrible symptoms: _____ (2). The disease was highly contagious; and Boccaccio, an Italian writer, says that even the slightest contact with a diseased person could result in infection. Of course, _____ _____ _____. Nevertheless, the plague spread rapidly along overland trade routes until virtually the whole continent was infected (4).

Consequences of the Black Death included _____ _____. By the time the plague subsided in 1351, roughly one-third of Western Europe's population had been wiped out. Individual populations decreased by millions over a few years. For example, _____ _____ (6). The confusion and fear that resulted from so much death led to rash accusations. In some places, Jews were blamed for the Black Death. Throughout Germany, _____ _____ (3). Pieter Bruegel depicted _____in his painting "Triumph of Death" by showing _____ _____ (5). According to Bruegel's masterpiece, the plague struck men and women, rich and poor, adults and children, and members of the clergy. No one was safe. Of course, Bruegel made this painting in 1562, centuries after the epidemic in 1347 had subsided, so _____ _____.

Between 1347 and 1351, the Black Death _____
_____. By 1351, one-third of
Western Europe's entire population had been wiped out by the plague and
_____. Useful additional texts
could include _____.

Finally, you can help students who are struggling with grammar, having trouble articulating their thoughts, or otherwise experiencing difficulty writing essays by holding one-on-one help sessions before or after school. Beginning in November, I hold one-on-one help sessions for students who are struggling, and these help sessions have proven very effective. However, rather than have students write their essays on paper (as I would during class), I have them use the dry-erase board at the front of my classroom. That way, students can easily correct their mistakes and see their essays stretched out on the board in front of them. As we re-write their essays together, my students and I devote considerable time and effort to making sure that their writing is clear, concise, and coherent; that all transitions are smooth; and that spelling and grammatical errors are kept to a minimum. After a few weeks of one-on-one help, students always see noticeable and lasting improvements in their writing.

Summary

The Common Core State Standards place a great deal of emphasis on writing about nonfiction texts. In order to be college- and career-ready in the 21st century, the Standards say that students need to learn to "use writing as a way of offering and supporting opinions, demonstrating understanding of the subjects they are studying, and conveying real and imagined experiences and events." Students must learn to "appreciate that a key purpose of writing is to communicate clearly to an external, sometimes unfamiliar audience," and "adapt the form and content of their writing to accomplish a particular task and purpose." They must "develop the capacity to build knowledge on a subject through research projects and to respond analytically to literary and informational sources." To meet these goals, the Standards say that students must "devote significant time and effort to writing, producing numerous pieces over short and extended time frames throughout the year" (CCSSI, 2010).

Of course, just as learning to analyze and evaluate texts is a process, learning to write analytically is a process. Just because students have already learned to write (or have even been told by their parents or other teachers that they are great writers) does not mean that they know how to write *analytically*. Students must learn to write formally, as objectively as possible, and gather information from multiple sources. They must learn to organize their essays in a way that is appropriate for nonfiction writing, and they must learn to cite their sources when they use them as evidence to support a claim. While this may seem like something that many of us would only have asked our high school students to do in the past (or, at the very least, students at the secondary level), Common Core expects all of us, including elementary teachers, to begin teaching our students these skills.

Because few students are already adept at writing well-developed and well-organized essays, it is important for us to guide students through the essay-writing process one step at a time. The first step in teaching students to write a good, analytical essay is to show them how to write a thesis statement, the argument the writer will be defending in the body of the essay. The second step is to show students how to support their thesis with evidence, and the third step is to show them how to cite each one of their sources. Finally, we need to show students how to incorporate point of view into the body of their essay and teach them how to write a conclusion. There are a number of strategies we can use to help students learn how to write a good analytical essay; and, with practice, our students will master this skill.

How might you use the strategies in this chapter to get your students writing good analytical essays? Feel free to write your ideas down here:

_____
_____
_____
_____
_____
_____
_____
_____
_____
_____
_____
_____
_____
_____
_____
_____

References

Bettenson, H. & Maunder, C. (Eds.). (1999). *Documents of the Early Christian Church* (3rd ed.). Oxford: Oxford University Press.

Boccaccio, G. (1351 [1855]). *The Decameron* (trans. W.K. Kelly). London: Henry G. Bohn.

Bulliet, R., et al. (2001). *The Earth and Its Peoples: A Global History.* Boston: Houghton Mifflin.

Common Core State Standards Initiative (CCSSI). (2010, June). *Common Core State Standards for English Language Arts & Literacy in the History/Social Studies, Science, and Technical Subjects.* Retrieved from *www.corestandards.org/ELA-Literacy*

Dunnigan, J. & Nofi, A. (1994). *Medieval Life and the Hundred Years War.* DENO Partnership. Retrieved from *http://hyw.com/books/history/1_help_c.htm*

Janu, B.D. (2000). *Bring Out Your Dead! Recreating the Black Death in the Classroom.* Cary, IL: Bell, Book, and Camera Productions.

Lualdi, K.J. (Ed.). (2005). *Sources of the West: Peoples and Cultures: Vol. 1* (2nd ed.). Boston: Bedford/St. Martin's Press.

Marcus, J.R. (1938). *The Jew in the Medieval World: A Source Book, 315–1791.* New York: Union of American Hebrew Congregations.

CHAPTER 6
Evaluating Students' Responses to Text-Based Questions

An important step of the writing process is to provide students with feedback on their responses to text-based questions. Students need honest and immediate feedback from their teachers if they are to grow as thinkers and writers. However, evaluating students' responses to TBQs is sometimes as challenging for us as writing good responses is for students. This is especially true when we first begin to evaluate our students' writing. When I was a new teacher, it took me a very long time to evaluate my students' work. Sometimes, I spent more than 15 minutes on a single essay, and I was always concerned about my ability to grade essays accurately and consistently. However, when I began using a rubric to evaluate my students' work, I found that I was able to grade essays more quickly and with more accuracy and consistency.

Using Rubrics to Evaluate Students' Responses

Of course, there are any number of rubrics we can use to make grading students' writing as objective, accurate, and consistent as possible. In my AP world history classes, for example, I use a scoring guide like the one in Figure 6.1. In this rubric, students earn a point for each task they complete (or each skill they demonstrate).

Points are awarded for having an acceptable thesis statement; supporting that thesis with evidence from the texts; understanding the meaning of the texts; grouping texts in at least two ways; analyzing authors' point of view; and suggesting an additional type of text that might help students more completely answer the question. Additional points are awarded for writing comprehensive thesis statements; analyzing point of view in multiple texts; grouping texts in more than two ways; and so on. Students can earn up to 9 points for an exceptional response to the TBQ.

I use this rubric in my AP world history classes because it is similar to the rubric the College Board uses to evaluate my students' essays on the AP world history exam. However, this rubric is not just for AP (or even high school)

Grading Criteria	Points
Has an acceptable thesis statement	1
Addresses all of the texts and understands the meaning of all or all but one	1
Supports thesis with appropriate evidence from all or all but one text OR	2
Supports thesis with appropriate evidence from all but two texts	1
Analyzes point of view in at least two of the texts	1
Analyzes texts by grouping them in at least two ways	1
Identifies what perspective(s) or types of text are missing and suggests an additional text that would be useful for more completely answering the question	1
Does two or more of the following: Has a comprehensive thesis statement, analyzes point of view in more than two texts, groups the texts in more than two ways, or suggests more than one additional text that would be useful for answering the question	2
OR *Does one of the following*: Has a comprehensive thesis statement, analyzes point of view in more than two texts, groups the texts in more than two ways, or suggests more than one additional text that would be useful for answering the question	1
TOTAL POINTS	9

Figure 6.1 Sample Generic Rubric

Source: Grading criteria retrieved from *apcentral.collegeboard.com*

students. It can be used by teachers in all grades and content areas. However, we might modify the rubric as we need to in order to accommodate the experience and skill level of our students. In fact, I sometimes use a variation of this rubric in my other classes (including my non-advanced courses) as well.

Another generic rubric I have adopted for use in some of my classes is the one in Figure 6.2. The New York Department of Education uses this rubric to evaluate students' ability to write good document-based essays. Notice that this rubric takes a more holistic approach to grading students' work. Students do not earn a point for each task they complete (or each skill they demonstrate); instead, they are awarded points based on the overall quality of the essay. For example, a student might score a 3 because his or her essay is more descriptive than analytical. Personally, I believe the rubric in Figure 6.1 is easier for teachers to use and provides students with more specific feedback on their writing.

Score of 5:

- Thoroughly develops all aspects of the task evenly and in depth.
- Is more analytical than descriptive (analyzes, evaluates, and/or creates information).
- Richly supports the theme with many relevant facts, examples, and details.
- Demonstrates a logical and clear plan of organization; includes an introduction and a conclusion that are beyond a restatement of the theme.

Score of 4:

- Develops all aspects of the task but may do so somewhat unevenly.
- Is both descriptive and analytical (applies, analyzes, evaluates, and/or creates information).
- Supports the theme with relevant facts, examples, and details.
- Demonstrates a logical and clear plan of organization; includes an introduction and a conclusion that are beyond a restatement of the theme.

Score of 3:

- Develops all aspects of the task with little depth or develops most aspects of the task in some depth.
- Is more descriptive than analytical (applies, may analyze, and/or evaluate information).
- Includes some relevant facts, examples, and details; may include some minor inaccuracies.
- Demonstrates a satisfactory plan of organization; includes an introduction and a conclusion that may be a restatement of the theme.

Score of 2:

- Minimally develops all aspects of the task or develops some aspects of the task in some depth.
- Is primarily descriptive; may include faulty, weak, or isolated application or analysis.
- Includes few relevant facts, examples, and details; may include some inaccuracies.
- Demonstrates a general plan of organization; may lack focus; may contain digressions; may not clearly identify which aspect of the task is being addressed; may lack an introduction and/or a conclusion.

Score of 1:

- Minimally develops some aspects of the task.
- Is descriptive; may lack understanding, application, or analysis.
- Includes few relevant facts, examples, or details; may include inaccuracies.
- May demonstrate a weakness in organization; may lack focus; may contain digressions; may not clearly identify which aspect of the task is being addressed; may lack an introduction and/or a conclusion.

Score of 0:

Fails to develop the task or may only refer to the theme in a general way; OR includes no relevant facts, examples, or details; OR includes only the theme, task, or suggestions as copied from the test booklet; OR is illegible; OR is a blank paper.

Figure 6.2 Sample Generic Rubric

Source: http://www.p12.nysed.gov/assessment/ss/hs/rgsr-a.html/

I also believe the rubric in Figure 6.3 is easier to use than the rubric in Figure 6.2. The rubric in Figure 6.3 looks much like the rubric in Figure 6.1. However, I like it because it requires students to demonstrate command of the conventions of standard English. Students are awarded points for proper grammar and usage and penalized if their errors impede the reader's ability to understand the meaning of their essay. This rubric is similar to the rubric developed for the PARCC Assessment and is also aligned with the Common Core State Standards.

Though far from being identical, the rubrics in Figures 6.1, 6.2, and 6.3 are similar in their expectations for student performance. For instance, all three rubrics require students to write an acceptable thesis statement ("... includes an introduction and a conclusion that go beyond a restatement of the theme"),

Construct Measured	Grading Criteria	Points
Reading Comprehension	Accurately analyzes the text	1
	Cites appropriate textual evidence to support analysis	1
	Demonstrates a full understanding of complex ideas expressed in the text	1
Writing Development of Ideas	Addresses the prompt	1
	Uses clear and convincing reasoning, details, text-based evidence, and/or description	1
	Demonstrates purposeful coherence, clarity, and cohesion	1
Organization		1
Clarity of Language	Includes a strong introduction, conclusion, and logical, well-executed progression of ideas	1
Knowledge of Language and Convention	Uses descriptive words and phrases, sensory details, linking and transitional words, words to indicate tone, and/or domain-specific vocabulary	1
	Demonstrates command of the conventions of standard English. There are few spelling and/or grammatical errors	1
TOTAL	**POINTS**	**9**

Figure 6.3 Sample Generic Rubric

Source: Grading criteria retrieved from *parcconline.org*

support their thesis with strong textual evidence ("... supports the theme with many relevant facts, examples, and details"), analyze the texts, and logically organize their essays. These requirements for students' writing should be universal. Other requirements (like grouping texts in two or three ways or suggesting that an additional type of source be included in the TBQ) are requirements that may vary from one instructor (and one assessment) to another.

Of course, there are dozens of rubrics we can use to evaluate our students' work. If we want, we can choose to write our own. We do not have to use a rubric adopted by state or local governments or one that has been created for use on a specific assessment. However, we should use *some* rubric to evaluate students' responses—one that measures the degree to which students have mastered the analytical, synthesis, and evaluative skills they need in order to write a high-quality essay.

Assigning Grades to Students' Work

As you begin evaluating students' responses to text-based questions, remember that students may have difficulty earning all the points on the rubric right away. For this reason, you may want to assign a different grade to students' work at the beginning of the year than you do at the end of the year. What constitutes a score of 5, 4, 3, 2, or 1 should probably not change over time, but what constitutes an A, B, C, D, or F probably should. Evaluating students this way will keep them from becoming frustrated when their initial attempts at TBQ-writing do not yield the high grades they may have earned on "regular"

Essays 1–3	Essays 4–6	Essays 7–10
9 = 110 A+	9 = 110 A+	9 = 110 A+
8 = 100 A	8 = 100 A	8 = 100 A
7 = 95 A	7 = 92 A	7 = 90 A
6 = 90 A	6 = 85 B	6 = 80 B
5 = 85 B	5 = 74 C	5 = 70 C
4 = 80 B	4 = 65 D	4 = 60 D
3 = 75 C	3 = 58 F	3 = 50 F
2 = 70 C	2 = 51 F	2 = 40 F
1 = 65 D	1 = 45 F	1 = 30 F
0 = 60 D	0 = 37 F	0 = 20 F

Figure 6.4

Evaluating Students' Responses

Essays 1–3	Essays 4–6	Essays 7–10
5 = 100 A	5 = 100 A	5 = 100
4 = 90 A	4 = 90 A	4 = 80
3 = 85 B	3 = 80 B	3 = 60
2 = 80 B	2 = 70 C	2 = 40
1 = 75 C	1 = 60 D	1 = 20
0 = 70 C	0 = 50 F	0 = 0

Figure 6.5

essays they wrote in other classes. For example, you might choose to assign students the grades shown in Figure 6.4 for essays ranked 0 to 9 (if you are using the generic rubric depicted in Figure 6.1). Or you may wish to use the grades shown in Figure 6.5 for essays ranked 0 to 5 (if you are using the generic rubric depicted in Figure 6.2). Of course, these are just possibilities. Ultimately, you have to use your own professional judgment about what grades to assign your students' work. However, accounting for the learning curve that inevitably comes with TBQ-writing will encourage students to improve their analytical thinking and writing skills over time without making them worry too much about their grades.

Peer Grading

In addition to grading essays yourself, you can have students grade their own essays or the essays of one of their peers. Sometimes, I set aside four or five essays for my students to grade as a class. As my students review the essays that I have projected on the screen at the front of my classroom, I tell them to keep track of the points each essay earns on a copy of the rubric they have on their desk. Then, I ask my students to tell me how many points they awarded each essay and to identify each essay's specific strengths and weaknesses. Usually, I find that my students are tougher on each other than I am on them and they are on themselves. This exercise is very useful for helping students learn how to write essays that meet the requirements laid out in the rubric. Especially for those whose essays I selected for grading, it helps students recognize mistakes in their own writing and correct those mistakes in order to improve their scores.

Once students get the hang of grading essays as a class, you can begin to have them practice grading essays on their own (or, if they are not yet ready for this, with a partner). Of course, it is a good idea to circulate among the students as they work and ask them to justify the points they award each essay.

Summary

When it comes time to evaluate students' responses to text-based questions, we need to ensure that we do so accurately, objectively, and consistently. There are any number of generic rubrics we can use for this purpose (such as the rubrics depicted in Figures 6.1, 6.2, and 6.3). If we do not like any of these rubrics (or the many other rubrics available to us online), then we can certainly create our own. However, we should use *some* rubric to evaluate students' responses—one that measures students' ability to write a high-quality essay.

Of course, students are probably going to have difficulty earning high scores on their essays at first. For this reason, it may be a good idea to differentiate between what score(s) constitutes an "A" at the beginning of the year and what score(s) constitute an "A" at the end of the year. If a student earns a score of 5 out of 9 at the beginning of the year, we might choose to give him or her a "B." On the other hand, if he or she earns a score of 5 out of 9 at the end of the year, we might choose to give him or her a "C." Grading students this way will help ensure that they can grow as thinkers and writers without becoming too concerned about their grades. Obviously, we want to provide students with an incentive to improve as thinkers and writers without punishing them for lacking experience.

How do you plan to evaluate your students' responses to text-based questions? Feel free to write your ideas here:

_____
_____
_____
_____
_____
_____
_____
_____
_____
_____

Appendix
Common Core Exemplars for Informational Text

Grades K–1

Aliki (1962 [1989]). *My Five Senses.* New York: HarperCollins.
—— (1965). *A Weed Is A Flower: The Life of George Washington Carver.* New York: Prentice Hall.
Bulla, C.R. (1960 [2001]). *A Tree Is A Plant.* New York: HarperCollins.
Crews, D. (1980). *Truck.* New York: HarperCollins.
Dorros, A. (1991 [1993]). *Follow the Water from Brook to Ocean.* New York: HarperCollins.
Garden Helpers (2009, September). *National Geographic Young Explorers.*
Gibbons, G. (1984 [1987]). *Fire! Fire!* New York: HarperCollins.
Hoban, T. (1987). *I Read Signs.* New York: HarperCollins.
Hodgkins, F. & Kelley, T. (2007). *How People Learned to Fly.* New York: HarperCollins.
Hurd, E.H. (1962 [2000]). *Starfish.* New York: HarperCollins.
Jenkins, S. & and Page, R. (2003). *What Do You Do With A Tail Like This?* Orlando: Houghton Mifflin.
Llewellyn, C. (2002). *Earthworms.* New York: Franklin Watts.
Pfeffer, W. (2004). *From Seed to Pumpkin.* New York: HarperCollins.
Provensen, A. & Provensen, M. (1978 [2001]). *The Year at Maple Hill Farm.* New York: Simon & Schuster.
Rauzon, M. & Bix, C.O. (1994). *Water, Water Everywhere.* San Francisco: Sierra Club.
Reid, M.E. (1996). *Let's Find Out About Ice Cream.* New York: Scholastic.
Thomson, S.L. (2005 [2006]). *Amazing Whales!* New York: HarperCollins.
Wind Power (2009, November/December). *National Geographic Young Explorers.*

Grades 2–3

Aliki (1983 [1986]). *A Medieval Feast.* New York: HarperCollins.
—— (2003 [2005]). *Ah, Music!* New York: HarperCollins.

Appendix

Arnosky, J. (2008). *Wild Tracks! A Guide to Nature's Footprints.* New York: Sterling.

Beeler, S. (1998 [2001]). *Throw Your Tooth on the Roof: Tooth Traditions Around the World.* New York: Houghton Mifflin.

Coles, R. (1995). *The Story of Ruby Bridges.* New York: Scholastic.

D'Aluisio, F. (2008). *What the World Eats.* New York: Random House.

Davies, N. (2001). *Bat Loves the Night.* Cambridge, MA: Candlewick.

Deedy, C.A. (2009). *14 Cows for America.* Atlanta: Peachtree.

Einspruch, A. (2004). *Crittercam.* Washington, D.C.: National Geographic.

Floca, B. (2009). *Moonshot: The Flight of Apollo 11.* New York: Atheneum.

Freedman, R. (1987 [1989]). *Lincoln: A Photobiography.* New York: Houghton Mifflin.

Gibbons, G. (1991 [1993]). *From Seed to Plant.* New York: Holiday House.

Kudlinski, K.V. (2005). *Boy, Were We Wrong About Dinosaurs.* New York: Dutton.

Leonard, H. (1998). *Art Around the World.* New York: Rigby.

Mark, J. (2007). *The Museum Book: A Guide to Strange and Wonderful Collections.* Cambridge, MA: Candlewick.

Milton, J. (1993). *Bats: Creatures of the Night.* New York: Grosset & Dunlap.

Ruffin, F.E. (2000). *Martin Luther King and the March on Washington.* New York: Grosset & Dunlap.

Smith, D.J. (2002). *If the World Were a Village: A Book About the World's People.* Toronto: Kids Can Press.

St. George, J. (2000). *So You Want to Be President?* New York: Philomel.

Thomson, S.L. (2010). *Where Do Polar Bears Live?* New York: HarperCollins.

Wick, W. (1997). *A Drop of Water: A Book of Science and Wonder.* New York: Scholastic.

Grades 4–5

Banting, E. (2004). *England the Land.* New York: Crabtree.

Berger, M. (1992). *Discovering Mars: The Amazing Story of the Red Planet.* New York: Scholastic.

Buckmaster, H. (2010). Underground Railroad. *The New Book of Knowledge.* New York: Scholastic.

Carlisle, M.W. (1992). *Let's Investigate Marvelously Meaningful Maps.* New York: Barrons.

Cutler, N.G. (2009, September). Kenya's Long Dry Season. *Time for Kids.*

Hakim, J. (2005). *A History of US.* Oxford: Oxford University Press.

Hall, L. (2009, September). Seeing Eye to Eye. *National Geographic Explorer.*

Kavash, E.B. (2003, October). Ancient Mound Builders. *Cobblestone.*

Koscielniak, B. (2004). *About Time: A First Look at Time and Clocks*. Orlando: Houghton Mifflin.

Lauber, P. (1996). *Hurricanes: Earth's Mightiest Storms*. Hauppauge, New York: Scholastic.

Montgomery, S. (2006). *Quest for the Tree Kangaroo: An Expedition to the Cloud Forest of New Guinea*. Orlando: Houghton Mifflin.

Nelson, K. (2008). *We Are the Ship: The Story of Negro League Baseball*. New York: Jump at the Sun.

Otfinoski, S. (1996). *The Kid's Guide to Money: Earning It, Saving It, Spending It, Growing It, Sharing It*. New York: Scholastic.

Ronan, C.A. (2010). Telescopes. *The New Book of Knowledge*. New York: Scholastic.

Ruurs, M. (2005). *My Librarian Is A Camel: How Books Are Brought to Children Around the World*. Honesdale, PA: Boyds Mills Press.

Schleichert, E. (2002, June). Good Pet, Bad Pet. *Ranger Rick*.

Simon, S. (2006a). *Horses*. New York: HarperCollins.

—— (2006b). *Volcanoes*. New York: HarperCollins.

Wulffson, D. (2000). *Toys! Amazing Stories Behind Some Great Inventions*. New York: Henry Holt.

Grades 6–8

Adams, J. (1776 [2009]). Letter on Thomas Jefferson. In Zall, P.M. (Ed.). *Adams on Adams*. Lexington: University of Kentucky.

California Invasive Plant Council (2010). *Invasive Plant Inventory*.

Churchill, W. (1940). Blood, Toil, Tears, and Sweat: Address to Parliament on May 13th, 1940. In Safire, W. (Ed.). (2004). *Lend Me Your Ears: Great Speeches in History* (3rd ed.). New York: W.W. Norton.

Douglass, F. (1845). *Narrative of the Life of Frederick Douglass, An American Slave*. Boston: Anti-Slavery Office.

Elementary Particles (2010). *New Book of Popular Science*. New York: Scholastic.

Engelbert, P. (Ed.). (2009). Space Probe. *Astronomy & Space: From the Big Bang to the Big Crunch*. Farmington Hills, MI: Gale Cengage Learning.

Enzensberger, H.M. (1998). *The Number Devil: A Mathematical Adventure* (trans. M.H. Heim). New York: Henry Holt.

Freedman, R. (2006). *Freedom Walkers: The Story of the Montgomery Bus Boycott*. New York: Holiday House.

Greenberg, J. & Jordan, S. (2001). *Vincent Van Gogh: Portrait of An Artist*. New York: Random House.

Isaacson, P. (1993). *A Short Walk Through the Pyramids and through the World of Art*. New York: Knopf.

Katz, J. (2001). *Geeks: How Two Lost Boys Rode the Internet Out of Idaho*. New York: Broadway Books.

Lord, W. (1955). *A Night to Remember*. New York: Henry Holt.

Macaulay, D. (1973). *Cathedral: The Story of Its Construction*. Boston: Houghton Mifflin.

Mackay, D. (1987). *The Building of Manhattan*. New York: Harper & Row.

Monk, L.R. (2003). *Words We Live By: Your Annotated Guide to the Constitution*. New York: Hyperion.

Murphy, J. (1995). *The Great Fire*. New York: Scholastic.

Nagel, R.M. (Ed.). (2007). Geology. *UXL Encyclopedia of Science*. Farmington Hills: Gale Cengage Learning.

Partridge, E. (2002). *This Land Was Made for You and Me: The Life and Songs of Woody Guthrie*. New York: Viking.

Peterson, I. & Henderson, N. (2000). *Math Trek: Adventures in the Math Zone*. San Francisco: Jossey-Bass.

Petrosky, H. (2003, Autumn). The Evolution of the Grocery Bag. *American Scholar* 72(4).

Petry, A. (1955 [1983]). *Harriet Tubman: Conductor on the Underground Railroad*. New York: HarperCollins.

Steinback, J. (1962 [1997]). *Travels with Charley: In Search of America*. New York: Penguin.

United States (1787). *US Constitution*.

Grades 9–10

Angelou, M. (1969 [1970]). *I Know Why the Caged Bird Sings*. New York: Random House.

Bronowski, J. & Selsam, M. (1965). *Biography of An Atom*. New York: Harper.

Brown, D. (1970). *Bury My Heart At Wounded Knee: An Indian Story of the American West*. New York: Holt Reinhart Winston.

Cannon, A.J. (1926). Classifying the Stars. In Shapeley, H., & Payne, C.H. (Eds.). *The Universe of Stars*. Cambridge, MA: Harvard Observatory.

Connell, E.S. (1984 [1985]). *Son of the Morning Star: Custer and the Little Bighorn*. New York: Harper Perennial.

Dash, J. (2000). *The Longitude Prize*. New York: Farrar, Straus, and Giroux.

Devlin, K. (1999). *Life By the Numbers*. New York: John Wiley & Sons.

Euclid. (300 BCE [2005]). *Elements* (trans. R. Fitzpatrick). Austin: Richard Fitzpatrick.

Gombrich, E.H. (1995). *The Story of Art* (16th ed.). London: Phaidon.

Hakim, J. (2005). *The Story of Science: Newton at the Center.* Washington, D.C.: Smithsonian Books.

Hand, L. (1944). I Am An American Day Address.

Haskins, J. (1998). *Black, Blue, and Gray: African Americans in the Civil War.* New York: Simon & Schuster.

Henry, P. (1775). Speech to the Second Virginia Convention.

Hoose, P. (2004). *The Race to Save Lord God Bird.* New York: Farrar, Straus, and Giroux.

King, Jr., M.L. (1963a). I Have A Dream: Address Delivered at the March on Washington, D.C., for Civil Rights on August 28, 1963.

—— (1963b). Letter from Birmingham Jail. In *Why We Can't Wait.* (2000). New York: Signet Classics.

Kurlansky, M. (1997). *Cod: A Biography of the Fish That Changed the World.* New York: Walker.

Lincoln, A. (1863). Gettysburg Address.

—— (1865). Second Inaugural Address.

Mann, C. (2009). *Before Columbus: The Americas of 1491.* New York: Atheneum.

Nicastro, N. (2008). *Circumference: Eratosthenes and the Ancient Quest to Measure the Globe.* New York: St. Martin's Press.

Preston, R. (1995). *The Hot Zone: A Terrifying True Story.* New York: Anchor.

Quindlen, A. (2001, September 27). A Quilt of A Country. *Newsweek.*

Reagan, R. (1988). Address to Students at Moscow State University. In Ravitch, D. (Ed.). (2000). *The American Reader: Words that Moved A Nation* (2nd ed.). New York: HarperCollins.

Roosevelt, F.D. (1941). State of the Union Address.

Smith, M.C. (1950). *Remarks to the Senate in Support of a Declaration of Conscience.*

Thompson, W. (2004). *The Illustrated Book of Great Composers.* London: Anness.

U.S. Environmental Protection Agency & U.S. Department of Energy (2010). *Recommended Levels of Insualation.* Retrieved from www.energystar.gov/index.cfm?c=home_sealing.hm_improvement_insulation_table

Walker, J. (1985). Amusement Park Physics. *Roundabout: Readings from the Amateur Scientist in Scientific American.* New York: Scientific American.

Washington, G. (1796). Farewell Address.

Wiesel, E. (1986). Hope, Despair, and Memory. *Nobel Lectures in Peace: 1981–1990.* Singapore: World Scientific.

Grades 11–12

Amar, A.R. (2005). *America's Constitution: A Biography.* New York: Random House.

Anaya, R. (1995). Take the Tortillas Out of Your Poetry. *The Anaya Reader.* New York: Warner Books.

Appendix

Bell, J. (2007). *Mirror of the World: A New History of Art*. New York: Thames & Hudson.

Boorstin, D.J. (Ed.). (1966). *An American Primer*. Chicago: University of Chicago Press.

Calishain, T. & Dornfest, R. (2004). *Google Hacks: Tips and Tools for Smarter Searching* (2nd ed.). Sebastopol, CA: O'Reilly Media.

Chesterton, G.K. (1909). The Fallacy of Success. *Selected Essays*. London: Methuen.

Declaration of Sentiments By the Seneca Falls Conference. In Boorstin, D.J. (Ed.). *An American Primer*. Chicago: University of Chicago Press.

Douglass, F. (1852). What to the Slave Is the Fourth of July?: An Address Delivered in Rochester, New York, on 5 July 1862. *The Oxford Frederick Douglass Reader*. Oxford: Oxford University Press.

Emerson, R.W. (1857 [1996]). Society and Solitude. *Essays and Poems*. New York: Library of America.

Federal Reserve Bank of San Francisco (2009). FedViews.

Fischetti, M. (2007, April). Working Knowledge: Electronic Stability Control. *Scientific American*.

Gawande, A. (2009, June). The Cost Conundrum: Health Care Costs In McAllen, Texas. *The New Yorker*.

Gibbs, W.W. (2008, June). Untangling the Roots of Cancer. *Scientific American Special Edition*.

Gladwell, M. (2002). *The Tipping Point: How Little Things Can Make A Big Difference*. New York: Back Bay Books.

Hofstadter, R. (1948 [1974]). Abraham Lincoln and the Self-Made Myth. *The American Political Tradition and the Men Who Made It*. New York: Vintage.

Jefferson, T. (1776). The Declaration of Independence.

Kane, G. (2005, December). The Mysteries of Mass. *Scientific American Special Edition*.

Kurzweil, R. (2008, January). The Coming Merger of Mind and Machine. *Scientific American Special Edition*.

Lagemann, E.C. (1991). Education. In Foner, E., & Garraty, J. (Eds.). *The Reader's Companion to American History*. New York: Houghton Mifflin.

McCullough, D. (2005). *1776*. New York: Simon & Schuster.

McPherson, J.M. (1994 [1995]). *What They Fought For: 1861–1865*. New York: Anchor.

Mencken, H.L. (1938). *The American Language* (4th ed.). New York: Knopf.

Orwell, G. (1946 [2009]). Politics and the English Language. *All Art Is Propaganda: Critical Essays*. New York: Mariner.

Paine, T. (1776 [2005]). *Common Sense*. New York: Penguin.

Paulos, J.A. (1988). *Innumeracy: Mathematical Illiteracy and Its Consequences.* New York: Vintage.

Porter, H. (1865). Lee Surrenders to Grant, April 9th, 1865. In Colbert, D. (Ed.). 1998. *Eyewitness to America: 500 Years of American History in the Words of Those Who Saw It Happen.* New York: Vintage.

Ravitch, D. (Ed.). *The American Reader: Words that Moved A Nation* (2nd ed.). New York: HarperCollins.

Tan, A. (1990 [2003]). Mother Tongue. *The Opposite of Fate: Memories of A Writing Life.* New York: G.P. Putnam's Sons.

Thoreau, H.D. (1854 [1893]). *Walden.* Boston: Houghton.

Tocqueville, A. (1835). *Democracy In America* (trans. H. Reeve). London: Saunders & Otley.

Tyson, N. (2003, December). Gravity in Reverse: The Tale of Albert Einstein's Greatest Blunder. *Natural History* 112(10).

United States. (1791). The Bill of Rights.

United States General Services Administration (2007). *Executive Order 13423: Strengthening Federal Environmental, Energy, and Transportation Management.*

Wright, R. (1945 [1998]). *Black Boy.* New York: Harper Perennial.